REISER+UMEMOTO

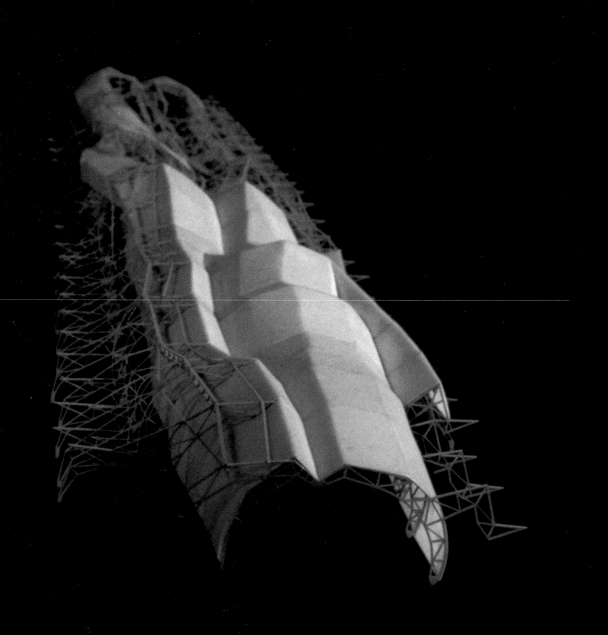

Andrew Benjamin

REISER + UMEMOTO

RECENT PROJECTS
Foreword by Daniel Libeskind

A.D. ACADEMY EDITIONS

Cover, page 1 and page 2: YOKOHAMA PORT TERMINAL competition entry

First published in Great Britain in 1998 by
ACADEMY EDITIONS

a division of
JOHN WILEY & SONS LTD
Baffins Lane
Chichester
West Sussex PO19 1UD

ISBN 0-471-97864-7

Other Wiley Editorial Offices
New York • Weinheim • Brisbane • Singapore • Toronto

Designed by christian@chkdesign.demon.co.uk
Printed and bound in Italy

CONTENTS

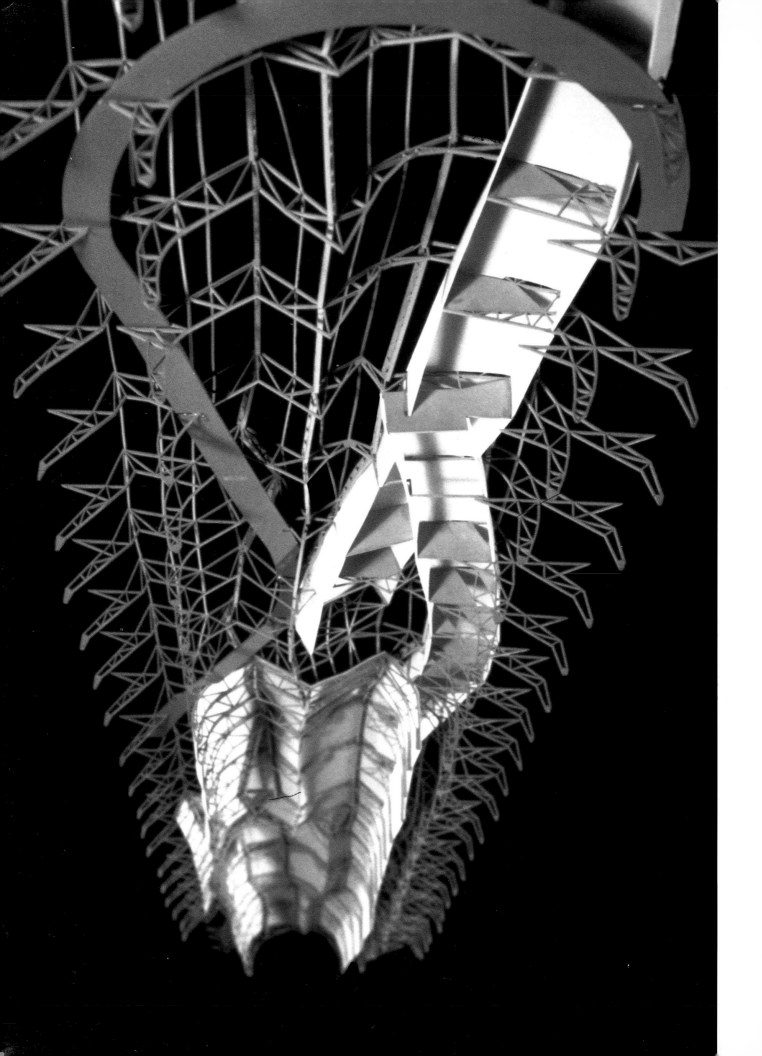

FOREWORD

Daniel Libeskind

By its very nature contemporary architectural practice exposes those whose aim is to conform to the political and the aesthetic situation of the field. Those who are involved in architecture usually enter it through a gateway called 'paradise'. They inevitably follow the logic of exemplarity. Whatever the style, the '-ism' or the theory, one can easily classify these philistines by the marketable objects they purvey. Today's architecture falls as easily into categories as the little spheres fall into the grooves of the pocket 'labyrinth' game. Those few who have another ambition – who think independently – have a vision that comes from some 'other' space, and are by and large relegated to the role of the dreamer, the theorist or the academic. They constitute the margin of architecture and their work is deemed an irrelevant supplement.

The collaborative work and vision of Jesse Reiser and Nanako Umemoto has little to do with the obvious architecture of today. As true innovators and original talents they have pursued a rare course of independence and imagination, oblivious to the slick market of images which pollutes the world. The course which they have travelled, risky as it may seem, is one of commitment to a tradition based on investigation, enquiry and craft. Unlike many contemporaries, who simply manipulate the 'givens' of architecture, and trade in objects, Reiser and Umemoto truly love architecture and contribute to its inner and vital resources. In the Talmudic tradition, the existence of the world at any time depends on the fact that there are Seventy Just Men supporting its reality. If an architectural survey were to be taken, Reiser and Umemoto would be one of the just. Their work adumbrates figures which come out of a shadowy existence and into a light not yet disturbed by reflection. The structures of their buildings refer to a melancholy, sombre and yet deep, ethical awareness which suggests that architecture of the future will not emerge gradually from a contemporary technique, but will burst forth suddenly, fully dressed in its ever-melancholic armour. The architect who opens the ever mysterious resources of architecture to new forms and possible techniques has always been a rarity.

Reiser and Umemoto's work is illuminating and insightful. It is characterised by an inventive constellation of amazing objects which raise questions about the chaotic disorder of institutionalised arrangements. Their dedication to enquiry, knowledge; their celebration of architecture deserve to be recognised and shared by a wide public. Reiser and Umemoto are destined to build on the basis of their already significant *œuvre*. They will undoubtedly bring to realisation in built form a renewed sensitivity for architecture's line, the deepened awareness of its shadows, and the construction of the paradoxical allegory which their work ultimately represents.

September 1997, Berlin.

Yokohama Port Terminal,
detail of main path (opposite)

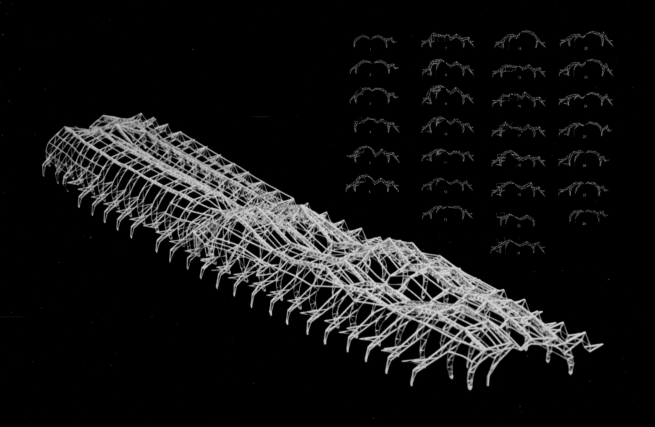

OPENING RESISTING FORMS

Recent Projects of Reiser+Umemoto

Andrew Benjamin

The architectural practice of Reiser and Umemoto has a direct impact upon architectural theory.[1] Yet theirs is not a theoretical architecture. It is rather that their own important innovations within architecture demand that particular response from architectural theory in which the theoretical must continually invent in order to respond to the insistence of their work. Work sets the measure for theory. In taking up the four projects – Yokohama Port Terminal, Cardiff Bay Opera House, Kansai Library and Bucharest 2000 – a sustained attempt has been made to stay with the projects themselves. These projects are situated at a vital moment within the development of the practice and the theory of architecture. In regard to practice it is not just the specific use made of technological innovations that is fundamental. It is rather that technology has provided the models in terms of which these innovations are to be understood, and, just as significantly, the computer has become a device that is inseparable from the design process itself. The development of complex surfaces, the shifts in how topology operates have become the work of animation and computer generation. Part of what marks out the significance of Reiser and Umemoto's work is that the engagement with the development of topology has not become an end in itself. In eschewing a certain formalism they have developed projects that open up the possibility of architectural interventions that resist a celebration of a simple novelty on the one hand and didacticism on the other.

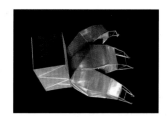

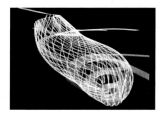

The full force of their work demands a larger setting. What has to be outlined is a context. The generality in question necessitates an identification of the contemporary in architecture. Within this setting it can be argued that there are, in their different forms, two concerns that mark the practice of architecture at the present. These concerns inevitably show themselves in different ways and with different results. In the first place, there is the possibility of avoiding the trap of mere novelty while still producing an architecture that is marked by its own version of 'alterity' – an otherness that defies an immediate reduction to a dominant tradition. (In the end these concerns will need to be formulated in terms of a complex structure of repetition.[2]) It is clear, of course, that there can always be a negative response to the question of alterity. Within it, conventions would be celebrated for their own sake and architecture could slide inexorably into building. Concerns with elegance and beauty, intermingled with what could emerge as a spurious conception of safety, would take the place of an affirmation of alterity and distance. And yet, because the inscription of alterity is neither automatic nor straightforwardly programmatic, what this will mean is that strategies marking out the process of alterity and distance need to be taken up with great care.[3]

The second concern pertains to what might be described as the problem of formalism. (A problem that can only be dealt with here in outline.) It is not as though architecture can escape a type of formalism. In the design process – e.g. the move from plan to section – there is a necessary and obvious formal dimension. Here, formalism presents itself in

Yokohama Port Terminal (opposite)
Cardiff Bay Opera House (top)
Kansai Library (middle)
Bucharest 2000 (bottom)

a different way and brings with it a different quality. The problem of formalism can be defined as emerging at that moment in a work in which formal innovation, and thus possible alterity, is promulgated in a way that intends to be indifferent to function.[4] Function will be introduced, but only as a predicate to an already formally construed subject. It is by tracing some of these concerns and their concurrent connection to the question of alterity that it will become possible to approach the recent work of Reiser and Umemoto. In order to take up that work it becomes essential to develop these opening considerations. Such a move needs to work through the projects. However, prior to that it is equally important to give what will be the register of their work a setting. In other words, further consideration must be given to the setting of architecture.

BUILDING ACTIVITY

Apart from itself what does architecture stage? Starting with a question means that a beginning can be made with a complex series of possibilities. The question, while allowing for a certain innocence – the presence of a question demanding an answer – will always be more demanding than it seems. In the first place, that demand hinges on the word 'stage'. Indeed, this word brings with it the setting in which the complex possibilities involved in the interpretation of architectural practice can be situated. Staging brings with it a number of openings. However, before discussing their important moments of difference and interconnection, it is essential to stay with staging. There is an element within all of these openings that will be similar. The similarity is activity. Staging – the staging at work in the question concerning what it is that architecture stages – involves activity, process and movement. Staging announces therefore the presence of an already existing economy; an economy that in opening up will yield the presence of differing economies. While it remains the case that activity, movement – thus the presence of economies – will all have to admit the differences that mark important divergences within the interpretation of architectural practice, it is vital, here, to remain with activity.

How then is the activity to be understood? To insist on the presence of activity, of the economic, within architecture, is not to insist on the primacy of construction. Rather, activity is linked to the built. And yet, despite the simplicity of this formulation it brings with it a complicating factor. As will emerge in greater detail in the argument to come, the built can only be understood with reference to time. Time inheres in building in different ways. (This set-up – *built time* – will be discussed in detail in the analyses to come.) Built time will always be present in terms of the way modalities of completion work within the building's own economy. Or, more specifically, it will be effective, at work, within the way certain conceptions – differing and perhaps incompatible conceptions – of historical time are operative within the structuration of different buildings. Regardless of the formulation that time will come to be given, it will have already been at work in the work of architecture. Working with the assumption that time is only present in particular determinations

– e.g. narrative time, filmic time – what marks out this project is that it starts with the recognition of the already connected presence of activity, architecture and time. These terms therefore – *activity, built time* – are interarticulated: their generality, which is under discussion in this instance, and their particularity, which will be taken up within a consideration of specific projects, open up the staging of architecture.

Activity becomes a way of describing both the presence of a building, as well as the presence of an urban field. However, what does it mean to describe a building as active, as having activity and thus as having its own economy? In general terms, the answer to this question is best provided by beginning with that which stands opposed to activity, namely the static, or the fixed. While the opposition should not be taken as straightforward, existing thereby as a simple either/or, it is nonetheless the case that the point of the contrast is between construing the object – the building, the urban field – in terms of either a dynamic process in which the object is taken as enacting, thus staging, its own project, or as given by a complete and self-present finality. In the latter case – the assumption of fixity – the object's meaning will be the locus of investigation. This will occur in the place of any concentration on the way form and function are interarticulated (their interarticulation entails that design becomes inseparable from function and thus programmatic considerations). Meaning locates the building within the domain of the visual, while process identifies the building's work as the work of architecture. In sum, with the assumption of fixity, the object is taken as a given, and as such an analysis of it becomes a description of the given, with the possible concomitant attempt to attribute a specific meaning to the object. In the case of the former – object as dynamic process – the object is attributed a project that it as an object seeks to realise. The object has a self-effecting presence; it seeks to realise itself. Effectuation is the movement involved. The utilisation of an expression such as 'seeks to realise' is intended to underscore the centrality of activity. Defining both activity and movement in relation to the object's work, and thus as internal to the object, is intended to re-enforce the attribution of an economy to the object.

Here, it is essential to be precise concerning what is meant by the object. There are two elements involved in the answer to the question of the object. In the first place, there is the specific architectural or urban object under consideration. In the second, there is the more exacting problem of how its being as an object is to be understood. It is in terms of this second consideration that activity and built time need to be positioned. As will become clear, however, the second comes to read back into the first; i.e. back through and thus into the particular object. The capacity for its being able to be read back in will entail that it was already a part of the particular object. Indeed, in a sense, it will have already been central to any investigation of the object's particularity.

What is being addressed in the second is the ontology of the object. It goes without saying that pragmatically what is under consideration is, for example, a specific building; a building which can be located within a given historical frame and to which functional and programmatic concerns can be attributed. While it is always possible both to interpret a given building in different ways and to attribute a range of differing symbolic meanings to it, it remains the case that in the act of interpretation, and in the attribution of a certain symbolic force, the ontology of the object – here the building – is only ever addressed tangentially. Meaning is privileged and thus the specificity of the architectural object – the being of the object *qua* object – remains unaddressed. Architecture is reduced therefore to the symbolic presence of the object.[5] There is no suggestion here that a building or urban condition do not have or should not have a symbolic dimension.

All that is being questioned is the identification of architecture with the building's symbolic register. In sum, the symbolic is equated with the ontological. (The existence of the object is its existence as a symbol.) The question is therefore, what is involved in addressing the ontological directly? There has already been a preliminary attempt to answer this question. What has to be recognised is that the contrast between the static and the fixed on one side, and process and becoming on the other, should not be understood as a simple choice – a choice with the same ontological setting. The difference cannot be therefore thought of in terms of variety. Moreover, it cannot be understood as allowing for a form of reduction in which the elements comprising the differences could themselves be explicated in terms of a founding unity. The distinction has to be understood as ontological in nature. What this entails is that the distinction – a difference resisting reduction – has to be described in terms of a differential ontology. In other words, it is a distinction concerning two different, and in the end irreducible ways of explicating the differing modes of being proper to the object – here the building.

Stasis and becoming do not comprise a divide that separates buildings and urban fields. They mark out the presence of different ways of construing what is ostensibly the 'same' object. It is only within the terms set by the construed object itself that it becomes possible to generate differences between types of architectural practice. The force of the difference lies in the way that time figures within the object's formulation.

Once activity is taken as central and the object explained in terms of its attempt to realise its own project, then not only does this eliminate the intrusion of a new formalism, this elimination becomes a necessary consequence of inscribing function as central to the object. It is, after all, function that the building seeks to realise. An argument against this position would have to assume the viability of the proposition that architecture could create a value-free and hence neutral space that simply awaited functional or programmatic considerations. As will emerge from the work investigated here, not only is that impossible, but the real force of the capacity of the yet-to-be that will be developed in outline here in terms of the incomplete, only emerges when it is indissolubly linked to functional concerns. To the extent that functional concerns are taken as central to any consideration of the object – again function as an integral part of the object's self-effectuation – this will have two important consequences. The first will be an opening up of function. The second concerns activity and the building's economy; the latter, however, is linked to the former as it brings with it the complex interconnection between function and design.

The interconnection has two significant elements. On the one hand, once function is understood as always already integral to the design process then any engagement with function will have to bring with it an engagement with design. And yet, on the other hand, there is also the important corollary that a simple change on the level of design will not entail an examination, let alone a shift in how function is understood and is thus present. In other words, if there is an engagement with function then that will have design implications. However, innovation on the level of design may leave function unaddressed. This latter possibility will almost inevitably arise from the situation in which design is thought not to have direct functional or programmatic implications.[6]

There is an inevitable risk in using a term such as function. It is often taken as unidimensional. The break with function therefore is thought to be a break with function itself, when in fact such a conception of the break positions function as unidimensional in order that the break be effected. Not only does this fail to understand the nature of function, such a position often brings with it, as has been intimated, a commitment, no matter how implicitly stated, of a space independent of functional and programmatic considerations. Because of the complexity and the difficulty of this position it is vital to move slowly. Function is not given within an either/or. (Either there is the function or there is the appearance of the functionally neutral.) Moreover, the imposition of function is inescapable. There are two questions here. What is meant by the presence of the inescapable? What occurs in the break from a unidimensional conception of function? The key to both these questions is repetition.

Within any designed space, there may be space awaiting the injection of programme; and therefore such a space must have the status of the yet-to-be programmed. Within any designated building the functional may not have an exact relation to design. In the slippage there may be functional concerns that are also marked by this yet-to-be. However, the setting in which these futural projections occur is the object itself. In other words, the future is conditioned by the nature of the present. Moreover, it is conditioned by the retention, the necessary retention, of the function that the building seeks to realise. It is thus that there is an inescapability of function. Furthermore, what makes functional concerns inescapable is that function is already specific. There are in fact only functions; functions which are repeated within any new instance of a specific and thus functional building. What is repeated is not the unidimensional nature of function but the dominant conception that a particular function will have, and thus the way in which the design process must allow for the relatively unproblematic repetition of that function.

The inescapable therefore is the inescapability of repetition. The apparent unidimensionality of function is simply that interarticulation of design and function enabling the repetition of dominance. Once the object is construed in terms of activity then the logic of the building – the building's own economy – will concern the nature of its relationship to repetition. The inescapability of repetition generates both a site of judgement and the locus of intervention. It will be in terms of this setting that invention needs to be positioned. Invention cannot be disassociated from the work of repetition. Even if there are only functions, even within a delineated function – e.g. a library – there is both a possible repetition of dominance, the dominant configuration of technology, power and knowledge, or a repetition in which the function of the library is only held in place to the extent that the function is transformed. The transformation is effected by design but is only successful because of the secured centrality of a function to be transformed. Intervention and invention combine in that they become repetition's other possibility. Detailing this position means linking it to what has already been identified as built time.

DEVELOPING BUILT TIME
Writing of a specific project – his own design for the Cardiff Bay Opera House – Greg Lynn reformulated what he identifies as 'novelty' in the following terms: 'Novelty, rather

14 than an extrinsic effect, can be conceived as the catalyst of new and *unforeseeable* organizations that proceed from the interaction between freely differentiating systems and their incorporation of external constraints.'[7] (My emphasis.) While it will always be essential to return to the detail of this claim, its initial importance is its location of that which is yet to be seen. Even though it can be attributed to generality, insofar as his argument could also concern the interaction of general systems or the interaction of systems removed from the particularity of a specific object, it has additional purchase when it comes to the description of particularity, since it can be further argued that what he identifies as 'interaction' could in fact be a description of the generation of particularity itself. There is no reason to believe that particularity cannot pertain either to the building or to the urban field.

Part of the force of this description is that it brings the future, here identified as the 'unforeseeable', into play. There is an inscription of the future. However, it is not an inscription that is in any way futuristic, if the future is merely a posited and often utopian counter to the present. Lynn's argument involves the inscription of the future within the present. In this instance, the future occurs and is thus present within the organisation of the present. Once the future becomes a condition of the present, then the present becomes a complex and irreducible site. The present resists the possibility of its being present to itself. It is, of course, in terms of the future that it is possible to differentiate between conceptions of activity. Moreover, the inscription of the future – the yet-to-be – will mark the presence of a different economy than one concerned with closing down the future or giving it a precise determination in terms of reuse. The inherent conceptual difficulty of this position, at this stage, must be allowed to endure.

A similar temporal organisation is evident in John Rajchman's engagement with the question of the new within architecture. Addressing this question he argues that: ' ... the avant-garde wished to resolve the tension between art and technological necessity by displaying 'function' in visible form, rather than trying to expose in given forms the tension with function that is the chance of the *invention to come*.'[8] (My emphasis.) For Rajchman the limit of what he identifies as the 'avant-garde' is that its project works by closing the temporal gap between form and function so that one is incorporated within the other. It is as though form becomes the representation of function. Here, completion is not simply a structural question it is equally a temporal one. However, there are two different temporalities at stake. In contradistinction to the temporal closure – a set up that demands the excision of deferral and thus a relation of immediacy between form and function – there is a time that works between immediate closure and pure openness.

In working between them it becomes a conception of temporality that resists the opposition between closure and openness. As such, rather than demanding that the presence of one exclude the other they become co-present – co-present in their difference – within the object. Indeed, it will be in terms of their co-presence that the opposition comes to be transformed. In the place of an excluding opposition between closure and openness, there is the productive interplay of the complete and the incomplete. Both terms will designate different ways in which design and function are interarticulated.

What this entails is that an opening emerges which is other than a simple middle point. The relation will involve greater complexity. Indeed, it will be that complex relation between architecture and time that insists within Rajchman's formulation of an 'invention to come' or in what Lynn identifies by the 'unforeseeable'. What renders these formulations complex is that within them space is either yet to be formed, or formed as indeterminate. These possibilities, which become the inscription of a temporality of the incomplete into the economy of the building, are formed within the project such that they work to inform the programme. The importance of Lynn's description of this state of affairs is that his recognition of the importance of constraints and thus the necessity not to accept any one determination of a constraint as a *fait accompli* works to avoid the possibility of a merely formal innovation. This recognition is also at work in Rajchman's formulation. When he links 'invention' to a 'tension with function', then the important question concerns how it is that function is retained within and as part of that site of tension. While this is a fundamental question, what it retains as its premise, though perhaps, more emphatically, as its condition of possibility, is the further consequence that 'invention' is only possible because of function's retention.

Before turning to the projects themselves it is essential to take up the incomplete. Again, while allowing for the retention of generality, it is essential to reiterate that what is involved here is the incomplete within architecture. Defining it in this way means that the incomplete has to be linked to what has emerged thus far concerning activity and built time. In sum, the incomplete can only be thought of in relation to the way repetition works within the production of architecture.

In general terms the incomplete becomes a way of holding on to the presence of function, while at the same time holding open the precise nature and thus the realisation of that function. The building becomes an unmasterable site precisely because the already present determinations, demanded by the slogan of 'form follows function', have themselves been opened up. Opening up the tight interconnection inherent in that demand yields neither the appearance of neutrality – function as the 'afunctional' – nor the utopian. What emerges is that which will be present in terms of the yet-to-be. However this possibility is, as has already been indicated, the inscription of the future into the present. The unmasterability of that inscription – and it is an inscription realised by the formal practice of architecture – yields the opening that allows for the possibility of alterity in architecture; other times and other buildings.

The incomplete depends upon the complete. The latter is finitude, the former is the potential infinite defined in relation to that finitude. In pragmatic terms the incomplete is an immaterial effect inscribed in the building's work and having a material source. Terms such as finite and infinite need to be taken as temporal terms. An architecture that seeks to close down the potential opening and questioning of function achieves this end by attempting to exclude the incomplete and thereby to create a work determined by self-control and self-presence. Mastery excludes the place of a productive opening by its retention of determined prediction; it is retained in the place of chance. Allowing for the incomplete and therefore a retained immaterial presence is, once more, to allow for alterity and distance within architecture.

Temporal complexity governs the economy of Reiser and Umemoto's Yokohama Port Terminal project. Not only will there be the temporality of the incomplete, which will be connected to the already present temporal distinction envisaged in the project's use. The passage of ships and the use of the terminal as a port will involve a different rhythm than the everyday use of the site occasioned by the presence of gardens and other activity areas. What needs to be pursued is the relation between these differing forms of time. As a preliminary move, however, the differences between the conventions of shed building need to be distinguished from what was proposed for the port terminal. These two sets of temporal distinctions are interconnected. Difference within programme is sustained by the building's own productive economy. Articulating the difference with shed construction will necessitate returning to the productive presence of time; in other words, it will demand specifying the way built time can be linked to the incomplete and to that extent enjoins alterity by giving it a formal presence. It should not be thought, however, that built time is connected only to the incomplete; as will be suggested, built time is equally as operative in the claim that the nineteenth-century shed is enacted within – and to that extent enacts – a temporality of determined completion. In other words, determined completion is another form of built time.

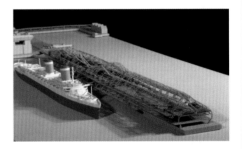

In their own description of the project Reiser and Umemoto refer to the differing senses of the incomplete operative within the work. What can be taken as incomplete is present in both the concept governing the project and in the way the envisaged structure would work to enact it.[9] In regard to the latter their position is articulated in relation to the tradition of shed building. What guides the tradition is the creation of uniformity. The structure would have to sustain and maintain a spatial dimension that admitted only one determination. As homogeneity should not just be a description of the space, but will also have been maintained by the work of the overall structure, framing should work to create a

Yokohama Port Terminal (above and below)

space articulating a repetition of the Same. Within this particular repetition – and it is clear that it is a repetition that is structural as much as it is conceptual – built time is presented as both totality and finality. Homogeneity, while spatial, admits a temporal description insofar as the nineteenth-century shed is marked out by the interplay between spatial homogeneity and temporal finality. The importance of insisting on this interplay is that it produces the site in which it will become possible to position distancing as yielding the place of alterity. In other words, it yields the site of both intervention and invention.

Countering this conception of built time could be envisaged as dividing up the internal area in such a way so as to introduce apparent complexity. However, the complexity in question would have been simply quantitative in nature. It would have been as though the greater the divisions within a single space, then the greater the degree of complexity. Not only does such a position misconstrue the nature of complexity, it would entail in the end that complexity was no more than a form of confusion. The question, therefore, is what is involved in the introduction of complexity once it is no longer understood as quantitative in nature?

Answering this question on a general level would assert that complexity is only possible once there is a founding irreducibility, and where the irreducible is explicable in ontological and temporal terms. As such, the mark of a complex would be the co-presence of the complete and the incomplete or the material and the immaterial. Complexity becomes the affirmed presence of a plural event.[10] The difficulty is that as this is not a theoretical or general claim that can only be instantiated in one specific form, then the move to the specific has to hold to the insistence of particularity. In fact, particularity can be defined as precisely that relation between the plural event and its affirmed specific presence. It is thus that there can be no architecture of the present – as opposed to building – without the event. The nineteenth-century shed can be taken as attempting to eliminate the possibility of a founding complexity by eliminating the incomplete. As such, particularity would have been effaced by the drive for a repetitive continuity of the self-same. The response to this drive – what would amount to an intervention into this form of repetition – would necessitate a disruption that is the intrusion of other spatial possibilities. Reiser and Umemoto refer to this disruption in terms of 'perturbation' and 'transformations'.

Different forms of development are envisaged within the overall structure. These disruptions are made possible by the initial use of a determined structural model. Rather than an overall homogeneous structure with its own surface – maintaining the received conditions of inside/outside and surface/depth – the incorporation of the possibility of differential growth stemming from the specific use of the three-hinged arch allows for mutations that overcome the idea of linear development. Spacing works by working through spaces. Part of the project's own activity is its effecting spacing. This would occur by the way in which the reiteration of the building would, in the addition of further elements, create additional spaces and thus sites within the overall structure which are, of course, envisaged as already being part of the structure. A way of describing this conception of addition would be to formulate it in the following terms: x + y = x + y + z. In the case of the tradition of shed building, the addition of 'y' to 'x' would be straightforwardly 'x + y'. In this instance the addition of 'z' has to be understood as the unpredictable consequence of adding 'y' to 'x'. What will be known henceforth as the 'z factor' is a created space that is always internal to the object. While it is always mediated by the function of the object, it nonetheless opens up programmatic

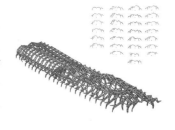

Yokohama Port Terminal, structural skeleton

18 possibilities that cannot have been predicated. Again, this has to be understood as the inscription of the future into the present. Accounting for the 'z factor' has to involve a detailed account of how surfaces contain depths that eschew the automatic functional control of the flat surface. Depth need not be taken literally. It is rather that depth, in this instance, attests to the presence of a complex surface and therefore needs to be understood as important development within topology.

In this specific case this system will also work both to integrate the two elements of the building – port and community space – while simultaneously holding them apart. Moreover, the generation, a surface that is not just the roof but a roof having its own depth and thus a differential structure that is itself self-generated by the process that yields part of the interior space, allows for different permutations of the surface and thus of its possible use.

The important element is that the reiteration of the frame – a reiteration generating and inscribing difference – allows the structure to work by distancing the hold of a simple syntax by yielding areas and thus spaces that work to determine the nature of the programme specifically because they can be described as the 'unforeseeable organisations' whose use and thus whose function will always have to be negotiated. The presence of the yet-to-be in this instance would be generated by the building's own self-realisation and thus would be integral to its operation and activity as a building. (Again, what has to be noted is the interplay of activity and built time.) The economy in question would have inscribed the possibility of an 'invention to come' within its own practice. What emerges, therefore, is an opening for a building that will demand its own theoretical response. Demands are made once the site of repetition demands another form – and almost invariably this will be a productive form – of iterative activity.

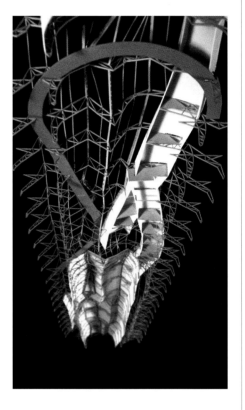

Yokohama Port Terminal, detail of main path

Finally, therefore, what occurs with this project can in the first instance be defined negatively. There is neither a repetition of a specific tradition within architecture, nor is there a purely speculative and utopian gesture. Secondly, there is the affirmative description. Guiding this description is the irruption of the unpredictable from that which is already present within architecture. There needs to be a different form of repetition. This repetition is not the presence of a ghost haunting the architectural nor is it merely the recognition of the uncanny – the uncanny, after all, leaves the initial house intact. There must be a twofold movement that is both an extrusion and intrusion. It is this state of affairs that is identified by Stan Allen in terms of the task: ' ... to define a sustainable project of creative work, capable of perturbing existing categories by the production of something unrecognisable out of that which is all too familiar.'[11]

The negative and the positive description are imbricated. What is created by their overlap is the space to come in the precise sense that it is the space which is already there. This affirmation of the presence of the future within the present is one of the dominant motifs of Reiser and Umemoto's architectural projects. Indeed, it is that which will work to define the operation of built time in their projects.

This project concerns the event of architecture. Not the event of a building, but a building as an occurrence within the urban fabric. In other words, what determines this project is a refusal to position the building as independent of its setting. Yet, on the other hand, it cannot be suggested that the project is driven by a simple contextualism. It is rather that what allows for the positioning of the opera house is the attribution of a quality in which it forms part of the infrastructure of the Cardiff Bay area. What this means is initially difficult to explicate and therefore it is easier to define the project in the negative. Initially, what this positioning entails is that instead of viewing the building as self-enclosed, and therefore only present in term of its relation to its own context, the building takes on the quality of the context, thereby transforming what is meant by context. (It is this twofold movement involving transformation that is part of what marks out the power of this project.) While specificity is held in place – it remains an opera house – the question of how it relates to its context is resisted by its lack of indifference to its context. As they indicate in their own project notes, Reiser and Umemoto understand this play with context as a way of avoiding positing a singular building that would then become a separate and individuated cultural monument. (As will be seen, this link to the problem of the monument is also central to their conception of the Bucharest 2000 project.)

There are two aspects of this project that need to be pursued. The first is the detail of how the building works as infrastructure. The second is the way this happens as a direct result of the building's design. These two elements are related since it is the use of what they call a 'geodetic bag' that enables the first to work. In their own description of the geodetic they note that: 'In an architectural context ... with the interest in structural systems that could engender complexity through flexibility, geodetics becomes interesting precisely because as a system, it is capable of adapting to complex spatial formations without a corresponding increase in the complexity of the system.'[12] While it may be necessary to equivocate over the use of the word complexity, since 'complexity of the system' may involve a different sense of complexity than the one engendered 'through flexibility', it remains the case that what this formulation envisages is a geometry that will enable, in this instance, a series of relations between the inside and the outside, and between different parts of the building, that will be both absolute yet porous. Programmatic specificity is maintained despite the centrality of movement, defining occupation and thus experience within the building. This contributes to an initial understanding of how the building inscribes and to that extent repeats the set-up proper to infrastructure rather than the set-up proper to the isolated, and therefore isolating, cultural monument.

The consequence of the use of a geodetic structural system is that it is able to bear different elements and thus provide different surface effects. It is this provision that reworks the oppositions inside/outside and separate/combined. In, for example, the envisaged concourse and foyer area, the capacity of the surface to bear difference, while remaining structurally the same, means that it would be possible to allow for a continuity between foyer and auditorium without that continuity having a determining impact on the different programmatic demands specific to each. Entry into the building from the piazza, then to concourse, foyer and auditorium, is smooth despite the insistence of programmatic differences. Again, this is the effect of the capacity of the geodetic structure to bear differences. However, what is essential is the contrast. In other words, it is important to show what is being resisted with this structure.

Cardiff Bay Opera House, roof plan

Cardiff Bay Opera House, geodetic structural system

While it is difficult to generalise, it is nonetheless possible to envisage an opera house in which entry from the street leads directly into a foyer. The foyer opens on to a service area with drink and food provision, which in turn leads to the auditorium. This structure might vary on each floor – for example the upper-floor concourse areas might lead directly into the auditorium – nonetheless what would characterise such a set-up would be the necessity of a complete division between the different areas, and where the divisions within the building bore a more or less direct relationship to the geometry of the building. The separation of the different programmatic elements within the building would work to establish the presence of the building as singular and therefore as a potential monument. In addition, its internal divisions and thus its potential separateness would demand that it be viewed not as infrastructure but as existing in relation to a context. It would be in that relation that its potential monumentality would be realised.

Cardiff Bay Opera House, claw auditorium

It is vital to note that what enables the distancing of this set-up is neither a different conception of programming nor the intrusion of other ways of construing division within an already existing building form. The inscription of difference is an effect of the geometry. Tracing the work of the 'geodetic bag' through the exterior to the interior would be to follow the unfolding of a single surface which was able to generate differences. The creation of divisions that were neither open nor closed, positionings that were neither inside nor outside except at the extreme, are not the work of internal construction and thus the necessary effect of partitioning. This set-up is the creation – thus the effect – of a complex surface. It is the surface effect generating programmatic possibilities. As has already been intimated, positioning the building as a series of openings in which movement into it, through it and within it, defined, and in a certain sense generated, the building, works to rob it of the possibility of monumentality. This is not loss but a redefinition that occurs because these openings define the building itself as part of the activity that defines the urban setting. Access brings with it the flows and holds of the setting itself. This has the further effect of allowing for the retention of functional specificity; the building will work as an opera house, the complexity of the rehearsal hall further opens up a range of possible *theatrical* forms. However, function is retained beyond the hold of a certain conception of culture due to the integration of the building into a field of activity. It would have been integrated without becoming it. This is a direct consequence of a project that takes movement and activity as its point of departure.

Kansai Library,
image showing massing

KANSAI LIBRARY

How, today, is a library to be designed? What, today, is a library? While these questions can always be made more specific insofar as the type of library can be specified; the setting can be delineated; its relation to an already existing public as opposed to a private domain of activity can be adumbrated; it remains the case that with the question of the library there is a set-up in which the concerns of the present are already confronting

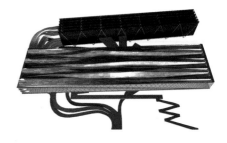

the complex relationship between technology and the storage and utilisation of knowledge. The library becomes the stage on which the relationship between knowledge and power is enacted with a singular force within this moment of modernity's unfolding. What then of the library? Answering this question will entail identifying what is specific about the Kansai Library project. It is the envisaged building's particularity that sets the stage for a return to the more general question of the library.

There are two interrelated strategies that can be identified in this particular project. The first involves the problem of storage and access. The second is the way that activity occurs within the library. Perhaps the most dramatic, and yet also the most simple, transformation that occurs in this project is the separation of these domains. The storage unit for books and documents is a building structured around efficient storage. Here, efficiency is not the existence of an archive resisting access. What is vital to the Stack Building is ease of the entry of material into the storage area and then the capacity to deploy those materials within the Library Building itself.

Kansai Library, interior view

The usual dilemma confronting the library concerns how to incorporate storage and public use within one building. Here it has been solved by having two buildings connected by an automated conveyor system. (Movement between the buildings is equally as important as movement within the Library Building itself. As will emerge, movement is productive.) While there are materials housed in the actual Library Building, its importance as a building arises because of its having been freed from the major problems of storage. As such, the question that arises concerns its activity as a building. Taking up this question brings design and function into connection. In order to emphasise the consequence of their design, it is helpful to contrast the building with a three-storey library in which the floors consist of distinct, unidimensional slabs and a building in which the connection between the floors is established via a public staircase and a semi-public elevator. While each floor could carry different programmatic possibilities, the system governing a particular possibility on the first floor could not, by definition, interconnect with a different system on another floor. The only way it would be possible to define a relationship between the floor slabs would be in terms of the stair case or the elevator. The interconnection would be between modes of access and the floors themselves. In other words, what comes to be precluded is the possible interconnection of what has already been identified as the 'interaction' of different systems. What guides Reiser and Umemoto's approach is that they wish to allow for this form of connection, with the consequence that the relationship between domains of the library can be brought about with the result of producing the unforeseen. In other words, the structuring of the design process is driven by the possible irruption, and hence interruption, of the 'z factor'.

It is this possibility that defines the way in which the internal operation of the Library Building would work. Instead of floors that are necessarily discrete there is an envisaged ramp system. The use of such a system redefines the spatial configurations across the ramp, the movement up and down the ramp and, from differing positions, one slab in relation to another. As with the Yokohama Port Terminal, the reworked relations are allowed for by the way in which the ramps function as a surface. What is excluded is unidimensionality. The difficult problem is trying to describe the differing ways in which it is excluded.

The use of a continuous prestressed steel roof would allow the ramps to be suspended. They are cut by vertical as well as horizontal modes of access. (It must be admitted, however, that with a ramp system, which in some senses generates a continuous surface, any straightforward conception of horizontality becomes problematic.) However, rather than the more conventional entry via either a stairwell or an elevator, differing points of entry allow the relationship between access and the place of access to become differing intersections with varying programmatic possibilities. The point of orientation has to start with the surface.

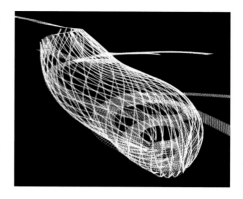

The floor space within a three-storey building within a unidimensional surface will only allow for differing programmatic possibilities that are given through addition and division. The area can be divided, the configuration of public and private space can be changed with addition of either temporary or permanent dividing walls. All these conceptions of change have to accept the building as complete, and thus it is this overriding sense of containment that delimits the range of the possible. In a general sense this is the surface effect of a what has already been described as a unidimensional surface. Moreover, in such a building there would be three different floor surfaces. (And yet, of course, while being different, it would be a difference defined and delimited by the work of the Same.) It is precisely this possibility that the ramp, which can be construed as continuous, resists, and, in resisting it, the way of utilising and working within the library comes to be transformed: an occurrence taking place on the level of building – the activity of the building – rather than on the level of meaning. Meaning emerges as a consequence of activity, since the transformation will have to do with the possibility that chance and the deferral of system may play an important role in how the relationship between technology, power and knowledge is understood. The plan for the Kansai Library project may come to present such a set-up. It would not symbolise it. Rather, such a possibility would be at work in the building's structure and thus in what would emerge as its economy.

Kansai Library, geodetic structure (top), elevation studies (middle and bottom)

The importance of a surface that resists the programmatic determinations, stemming from the unidimensional, is that rather than blurring distinctions between programmed areas, it allows their intersection to open up programmatic possibilities. This has to be understood as another version of the 'z factor'. If 'x' and 'y' are two programmatic possibilities with their own surface relations, then allowing for a surface structured by topological deformations is to allow for the overlap of 'x' and 'y', an overlap generated by the surface itself and in which 'z' is the consequence. It is not the consequence, necessarily, of blurred relations but of overlapping determinations. The overlap is not indifferent to the surface and therefore it is not indifferent to design. It is a consequence of the design itself and therefore part of the surface effect (a position which is the surface's effect). The emergence of the 'z factor' becomes the affirmation of a form of irreducibility. Once again, what this means is that the combination of $x + y = x + y + z$ takes on the status of a plural event: $x + y + z$ is a set-up that cannot be reduced to its constituent parts. It is therefore the mark of a founding irreducibility that has to be construed as productive and to that extent as a performative.

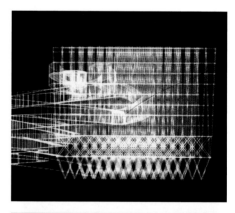

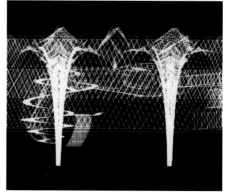

Finally, therefore, it is the consequence of this formulation that needs to be noted. The question of its import needs to be posed in relation to the library. The contrast has already been drawn between two different types of structure: one marked by a series of unidimensional floor slaps and the other utilising a continuous complex surface in order to generate unpredictable configurations. While this is a real distinction it remains merely formal unless the constraint of the library is introduced. Once that constraint is allowed to bear on the question of form, then, not only will there be the emergence of a different architectural configuration, it will also be the case that that difference will intrude into how the activity of research, the production of knowledge and the public/private distinction occurring within the institutionalisation of knowledge take place.

The site of innovation and intervention occurs to the extent that the presence of the library is held in place. However, the contrast is not between already determined conceptions of the library. The contrast is between a conception of finitude, and thus an architecture of the complete, on the one hand, and an inscribed openness dependent upon the interrelationship between the complete and the incomplete on the other. The presence of the incomplete will always be marked by the immaterial because it is the presence of the future – the continual opening up of the future – within the present. Again it is essential to be clear. The future in question is not the utopian other. The future is defined by the continual possibility of further 'unforeseen' functional and programmatic determinations sanctioned, in the instance, by the surface effect effecting the work of the incomplete. What this entails is that rather than assuming that the interplay of knowledge and power can only have one determined form – a form governed by a conception of totality in which each move is only ever an element of the totality – there can be the housed presence of the continual possibility, perhaps need, for inventions resisting absorption. This latter possibility is precisely what this conception of the Kansai Library is constrained to allow.

BUCHAREST 2000

Here, context is all. Not the 'provincial contextualism', which Reiser and Umemoto are right to dismiss in their own project description, but the context that awaits what they describe as the 'powerful forces of cultural and economic transformation engendered by a cosmopolitanizing infrastructure'. There cannot be any straightforward escape from the urban and architectural legacy of Nicolae Ceausescu's regime. It is, of course, the impossibility of escape that must be understood as central in this context. How, given what Reiser and Umemoto succinctly identify as 'an inflated monumental urbanism' is it possible for there to be another architecture and thus another urbanism? These demands, gesturing as they do to the problem of the other – another urbanism, another architecture – raise the important question of what will count as alterity within the architectural. It should not be forgotten that allowing for a date to have a determining role – here the year 2000 – introduces another aspect of otherness and another timing manoeuvre, neither of which can be reduced to the simple operation of chronology. Alterity does not exist *in vacuo*. On the contrary, it necessitates its own context. In this instance, the context is given twice. In the first instance, it is Bucharest. In the second, it is the presence of a monumental urbanism. It is this doubled context that generates the site. Moreover, it provides the orientation of Reiser and Umemoto's intervention. Theirs is an intervention within this site.

Again, it is possible to begin with a question. It will be a question that summarises the problem of alterity, but which recognises the insistence of the context; the context as twice given. The question is stark: how not to continue? Answering this question must

Bucharest 2000, site view

begin with what has already been given. Not only is there a given urban and architectural set-up; such a set-up is necessarily overdetermined. Responding must engage both with the empirical presence of what is there, as well as its overdetermined nature. What makes it overdetermined is that both the urban setting and its related buildings already have a monumental effect. Roads and buildings were intended to function as symbols. As such, there is an already present monumentality carried by the context. Moreover, it is a monumentality that is the consequence of destruction. Razing the inner city of Bucharest in order to create a monumental urbanism inscribes destruction at the heart of the enterprise. Responding to a particular form of destruction cannot occur as a simple reiteration of that act: a repetition of the Same. Hence the force of the question: how not to continue?

The project Bucharest 2000 involves an intervention and transformation of the main area of the city. Not only will there be the addition of infrastructure, there will also be introduction of axes through the area; through it, thus in part defining it. What guides the addition and the reworking of the road system is what has already been described as the doubled context. A direct way of addressing how an intervention into this site can occur is by starting with the central connecting route, Boulevard Unirii.[13] The symbolic importance of this route is clear. It defined a central procession, either to or away from what had been the Presidential Palace. The route was lined with new apartments blocks, all in a similar style and colour. They provided the perfect corridor through which to approach the palace. Their uniformity of style helped to control the eye. In fact, it is possible to argue that the procession, and thus the effect created by the approach, is structured by an envisaged uniformity of vision. In other words, the urban set-up can be understood as involving a twofold relation to sight. In the first instance, it is structured by the uniformity of vision, of what is to be seen. And in the second, it solicits the uniformity of vision; there is only one way of viewing what is to be seen. What the setting demands is a singular gaze. Moreover, it is in terms of this gaze that the monumental effect takes place. Countering an urbanism constructed around this conception of the gaze cannot involve proposing another object, as though the response should be the presence of another object demanding a similar conception of the gaze. In the first instance, the counter move must work within the site and in this sense it must work with the interconnection of movement, vision and the monumental.

The question guiding this analysis – how not to continue? – has to be precise. With what is continuity to be broken? The specification of a site generated by movement, vision and the monumental provides the locus of intervention. Allowing for other possibilities hinges therefore on being able to recast that which generates the site of intervention. In order to realise this possibility a distinction will have to drawn between the anti-monument and the process demonumentalisation. The analogy with myth is important here. If the counter to myth is a generalised demythologisation, does that necessitate a counter myth – here that

Bucharest 2000, site plan

would be the anti-monument – or does it involve a move that demythologises within a set-up that puts the mythic itself into abeyance? It is this latter possibility that is identified above as the process of demonumentalisation. Rather than the monument to the end of monuments there will need to be another way in. Preliminary to a further investigation of the three elements comprising the site of intervention attention needs to be paid to the consequence of precluding the anti-monument.

Perhaps the most important part of the legacy of Bucharest – a part that cannot be accounted for in any direct manner – is the role of destruction in the creation of the area of the city under consideration. Not continuing cannot escape the stricture of not destroying. To destroy may be no more than another way of continuing. What has to taken up, therefore, is another counter to destruction. While it may seem a paradoxical formulation, what becomes necessary is a way of giving expression to the presence of a discontinuous continuity. Continuity is at hand because of the refusal of destruction – and it here needs to be noted that what is being refused is the literal destruction of a series of buildings, roads and infrastructure created in the 1980s – while discontinuity is demanded by the imperative of not continuing. The anti-monument would arise as the result of having taken destruction literally. It would be for this reason that the rubble of destruction would have become the exemplary anti-monument. In this context, this would have been an inappropriate response for two reasons. In the first instance, it would have failed to grasp the central role played by vision in the construction of the original urban setting. The original setting allows for the description of it as monumental, precisely because of the uniformity of the gaze it demands. While in the second, such a response would have abandoned the strictures and the demands of architecture in the process.

Given that the Boulevard Unirii is a central axis within the city, what has to occur is a process of demonumentalisation, thought within the confines of a discontinuous continuity, that holds to the necessity of retaining the road. (Reiser and Umemoto refer to this type of possibility as 'an access that is not an axis'.) The same will also have to be the case with the buildings alongside the road. Equally, the former palace – now the House of Parliament – will need to be repositioned, even though it will also have to retain its current position.

Bucharest 2000, aerial view

In the case of the boulevard, the plan adopted by Reiser and Umemoto has two interrelated elements. Both are only explicable in terms of demonumentalisation. The first involves dropping most of the road beneath the surface. There is an elegant simplicity to this move. Once the road vanishes beneath the surface then its capacity to allow a uniformity of gaze has been transformed. The gaze within a tunnel will be devoid of any form of monumentality whatsoever. While eliminating the corridor will be essential to the general practice of demonumentalising, the surface remains. Here, in a move that reiterates part of the force of the Kansai Library project and Yokohama, in the place of a flat road the surface would now be a 'mounded park'. The force of the park is twofold. In first place, it would attract different types of programmatic possibilities, while at the same time it would eschew the possibility of the uniformity of the gaze. There would not be a single view. As such, the dominant dictate that controlled the original monumental construction would have been overcome, and yet this overcoming would have precluded the necessity of another monument. The counter to the monument – to the process of an urban monumentalism – need not create another monument. For the counter move, and here the counter needs to be envisaged as the instantiation of alterity, to remain architectural, it is almost essential that the construction of another monument be precluded.

The monumental nature of the palace, the second largest existing building (the Pentagon being the largest), comes to be incorporated into the other aspect fundamental to their project, namely a major loop system of roads. The importance of the road system is once again explicable in terms of the process of demonumentalisation. The loop works to establish connections between parts of the city that were initially separated after the destruction of the 1980s, in order to establish the original monumental structure. The palace would be linked to other buildings that would work to alter the scale of the original building. Its size would be mediated by its connection with previously separated parts of the city and by the development of an infrastructure, which would erode the singularity of the original palace by its incorporation within a growing infrastructure. While this aspect of the project would need to be developed in greater detail, its importance can nonetheless be situated in relation to the process of demonumentalisation.

In sum, therefore, what their submission to the Bucharest 2000 competition involves is a sustained attempt to reconfigure an urban setting utilising a series of strategies linked to the productive potential within demonumentalisation. Again, it can be seen that context, while not determining the nature of the outcome, sets the stage for the orientation of their intervention. The activity is not aimed at the elimination of the fabric's constituent parts. On the contrary, it is driven by the need to link growth to the advent of alterity. Their interplay – the productive presence of growth and alterity – opens up the possibility of an incomplete urbanism. What would make it incomplete is the twofold necessity of demonumentalising, while resisting the incursion of the counter monument. Such a point of departure precludes the possibility that there is a definite form proper to it. There is a continual opening to the extent that the incomplete is held as always in play within finite strategies. Finitude delimited by the work of the incomplete precludes representation, not because of representation's failure, but because their co-presence – the co-presence of the incomplete and the finite enacted as the plural event – precludes the presence to self and thus the self-completing finality demanded by representation. In not being one, there cannot be one thing to represent.

Bucharest 2000, aerial view

THE ENDS OF ARCHITECTURE

These projects can be attributed a specific end. Opening up that end will involve a return to what has already been identified as the staging of architecture. The key to any understanding of architecture being staged is repetition. And yet, because repetition cannot be attributed to either a singular form or an essential nature, it has to be more precisely understood as that which accounts for that staging. Since the new in architecture is always conditioned by that which has taken place, and thus because any architectural moment will already have been placed, architecture is repetition. Even if the architect forgets, the building will always remember its being as architecture. The central evaluative and interpretive question therefore will always concern the type of repetition that is being staged. What counts as a repetition in architecture cannot be distinguished from the recognition of the ineliminability of function. Function – always already inarticulated with its continually differing formal presence – is that which comes to be repeated in the staging of architecture. This defines the ends of architecture.

These ends are located within a structure of repetition in which there can be both an identification of the presence of that structure and the possibility that within the architecture's own effectuation, within its own activity as architecture, there can be a sustained engagement with that already present determination. In order for an engagement to take place, intervention and invention must occur within the prevailing structure of repetition. What has to be opened up is another staging of that which is given to be repeated. For this staging to eschew the incursion of the prescriptive and thus the closure that it brings with it, the present has to have the yet-to-be determined as part of its determination. Inscribing this quality, a quality that is primarily there as an immaterial effect, becomes the activity of the incomplete within architecture. It has the force of a productive negativity working as an opening within the present. And yet, as has already been suggested, this opening is not utopian. Rather than yielding a future that is beyond the present, the future is given as an already insistent possibility within and as part of the present. To the extent that this future is sustained, architecture maintains itself as incomplete. The incomplete is given in relation to an engagement with function that is realised by the activity of design. Form does not follow function. Form defines the possibility of alterity within function. This is architecture's other possibility. It is thus its other end.

Wolf Residence, landscape design
with Métier à Aubes

1 This text includes parts of an earlier study of Reiser and Umemoto's work, 'Not to Shed Complexity', *Fisuras*, December 1995, no 3, 1:4, pp46-57.

2 I have tried to analyse this structure of repetition in *The Plural Event*, Routledge (London), 1993, and in Chapter 1 of *Object Painting*, Academy Editions (London), 1994.

3 Stan Allen has investigated this problem with great precision. Rather than merely positing an architecture of distance – understood as being either utopian on the one hand or the conflation of architecture and building on the other – he has called for what he describes as 'an anexact fit between event and structure'. See his 'Dazed and Confused', *Assemblage* 27, August 1995, p53.

4 In a sense what is involved here concerns the new. How is the new in architecture to be understood? This is an extremely difficult question. This project – writing about the projects of Reiser and Umemoto – can be seen as an attempt to engage with that question. It is thus that it would be possible to begin to respond to another important recent paper by Stan Allen, 'From Object to Field', Peter Davidson and Donald L Bates (eds), Architecture After Geometry, *Architectural Design* Profile no 127, Academy Editions (London), 1997. While arguing for the viability of field conditions and signalling a return to a certain form of contextualism, he goes on to note that: 'Field conditions treats constraints as opportunity and moves away from a Modernist ethic – and aesthetics of transgression. Working with and not against the site, something new is produced by registering the complexity of the given.'(See p24.) It is clear that for modernism, transgression and the new are productively interrelated. The difficulty with Allen's formulation is not just that the new is not defined – though in the end that will have to be a problem – it is that 'registering the complexity of the given' may count as precisely an act of transgression for urban theorists who maintain a fidelity to the simplicity of the grid and then define the deviant – perhaps even the delirious – as being determined by it. Equally it will be a transgressive act if complexity means more than confusion.
   On a more theoretical level, it can be argued that such a registration would have to be a transformation of the given. It is unclear that the given is given as complex either phenomenologically or for the most part theoretically. Returning to the given would therefore involve a transformation or a transgression. In the same way as it is difficult to shake the hold of modernism, it is equally as difficult to force a radical divide between transgression and a conception of the new that falls beyond the reach of a celebration of simple novelty.

5 This is a complex and demanding point. It means, in part, that the attribution of meaning, where that involves an equation of meaning and the symbolic, represses the presence of the object and thus represses the presence of the ontological. However, it is also the case that it is the actual presence of what was identified above as the object *qua* object that allows the symbolic to function in the first place. The project here involves trying to trace the consequences of recognising their already present interarticulation.

6 This is, of course, the direct consequence of what has been called postmodern architecture.

7 Greg Lynn, 'The Renewed Novelty of Symmetry', *Assemblage* 26, April 1995, p11.

8 John Rajchman, 'What's New in Architecture', *Philosophical Events: Essays of the '80s*, Columbia University Press (New York), 1991, p162.

9 Even though it is a difficult point, the relationship between the concept and the structure, here, should not be understood instrumentally. Indeed instrumentality will always demand a more exact relation than their project allows. Incomplete relations will demand a theorisation that will have to operate outside of a simple oscillation between the presence and absence of instrumentality. The recognition of the state of affairs would serve to mediate the strictures advanced by Mark Wigley concerning a 'simplistic instrumentalisation of theory'. See his 'Story-Time', *Assemblage* 27, August 1995, p94.

10 I tried to develop this conception of the event in *The Plural Event*, 1993. See in addition my 'Event, Time, Repetition', *Columbia Documents of Architecture and Theory*, volume 4, 1995, pp139-49. The expression, plural event, is used in order to signal the presence of a founding irreducibility. However rather than the irreducible, identifying either variety of diversity, it has to be taken as ontologico-temporal in nature.

11 Stan Allen, 'Dazed and Confused', p54.

12 They have written extensively of their own use of the geodetic. The above quotation comes from the presentation of the Cardiff Bay project in *Assemblage* 26, April 1995, p36.

13 The range of issues involved in this project, and the difficult and complex background to it, mean that it is only possible to take up certains aspects of it. I have emphasised issues to do with monumentality. I am not for a moment suggesting either that is all that there is to Reiser and Umemoto's project, or that there are not other aspects that may not have been directly addressed by their submission to the contest. What differentiates this project from many others, however, is Reiser and Umemoto's acute recognition of the centrality of context.

Wolf Residence, Métier à Aubes

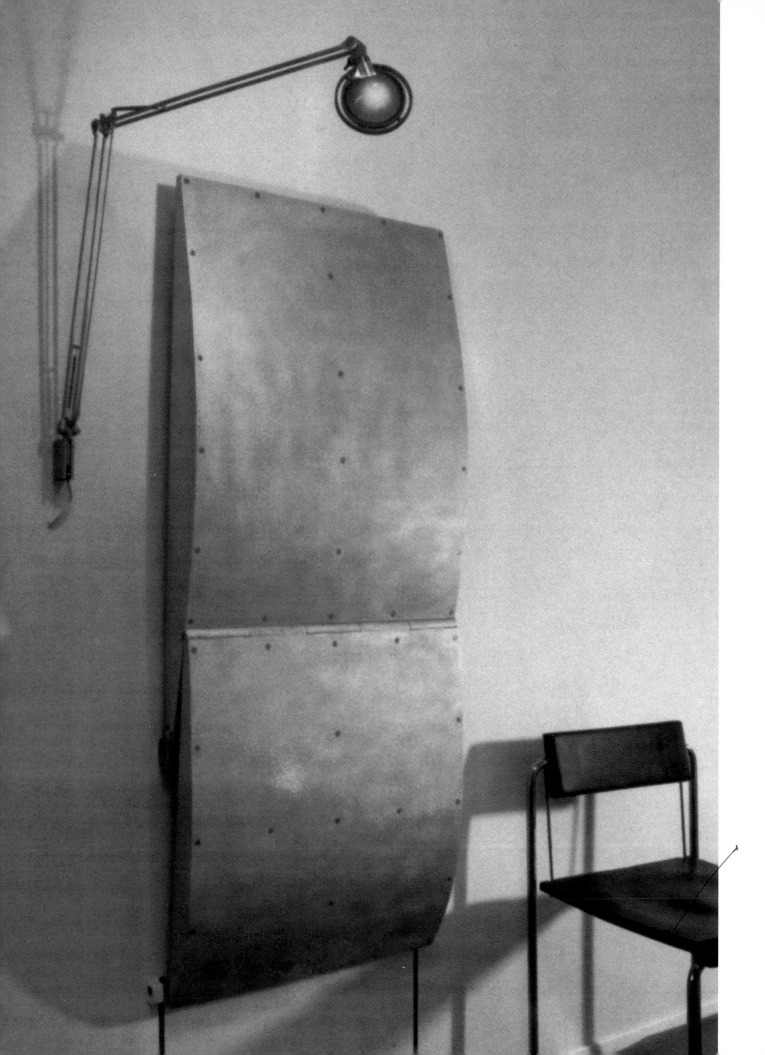

LOOSE FIT

Jesse Reiser

In place of the totalising systems of modernism, Reiser and Umemoto have pursued inquiries into chaotic or complex systems. These break with the main binary oppositions that have dominated architecture as a discipline: theory and practice; structure and ornament; global and local; and programme and form. The artificial static of old procedures is broken down and a new fluency and flux inserted in its place. In terms of programme and form, for instance, a new 'loose fit' is gained which focuses on the work in hand and its effects, rather than preordained conceptions of representation and issues of meaning.

Seventy-six years ago in the aftermath of the First World War, Paul Valéry, anticipating the triumph of the totalising ideologies of modernity, wrote:

> The world, which has given the name of 'progress' to its tendency towards a fatal precision, is seeking to unite the blessings of life with the advantages of death. A certain confusion still reigns; but yet a little while and all will be made clear; at last we shall behold the miracle of a strictly animal society, a perfect and final ant hill.[1]

This speculation was tragically borne out by the close of the Second World War, when modernism itself came to be implicated in the multiple horrors perpetrated by both the right and the left; these totalising conceptions are still very much with us – their reach and effects being exponentially greater than in 1945.

How then to respond specifically with the purview of architecture? To renounce systematicity in an effort to become nonideological, that is, to turn away from instrumental reason, is a stance of refusal, which at best renders one's architectural efforts ineffectual and at worst passively abets the consolidation of these totalising conceptions. This does not mean to imply that there is a direct connection between a particular system, political or otherwise, and a particular architectural form. Indeed, it is the very susceptibility of systems to transformation that suggests systematic inquiries into principles by which these transformations may be effected.

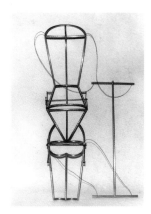

One promising line of development – which has begun to inform Reiser and Umemoto's work – has been the inquiry into chaotic or complex systems, especially in their capacity to engender new and unforeseen formations of programme, institutions and form. Central to this revaluation of system has been the attempt to rethink the nature and use of hierarchy in the design process, especially as it pertains to the complex exchanges between 'given' systems in a context and how these shade into those specific to the project itself.

In a discipline regulated by dualisms, four seem to crop up repeatedly. They are the assumed oppositions between: theory and practice; structure and ornament; the global and the local; and programme and form. The practice's task, like that of our colleagues, has entailed a loosening of these polarities, first and foremost, in the design process and later as conclusions. They are as follows:

1. Theory and practice: theory cannot be privileged. It is neither superior to, nor above, practice. Neither philosophy nor history can legitimate the work of the theory. Theory is not applied. On the contrary, theory occupies what Stan Allen describes as a 'horizontal relation' to practice.[2]

2. Structure and ornament: contrary to the classical formulation, ornament is not subservient to structure – rather, it is pre-eminently structure in itself; furthermore, that which would classically be understood as structure is an inherent subset to, and of, the general ornamental organisation.

Wing Table, foldable table for Bachelor's Apartment, New York City, 1993 (opposite)

Chaise-longue component for Métier à Aubes, Wolf Residence, Sands Point, New York, 1987 (above)

3. The global and the local: global systems of transport and exchange, and specific or local architectural proposals, have been understood (within modernism) as being in a mutually exclusive or dialectical relationship with one another. In response our architectural proposals implicate one in the other, and in so doing, attempt to bring about emergent or spontaneous events.

4. Programme and form: the loose fit between programme and form is acknowledged, and subsequently the lack of priority of the former over the latter. This can be summed up in the aphorism: 'programme is to architecture what the meaning of lyrics are to music'.

If we approach with caution any discussion of theory or method in direct relation to design, it is because linear developments, while convenient for the sake of argument, rarely fit so neatly or linearly 'in the event'. All too often, this apparent inevitability only becomes visible retrospectively, and thus appears preordained, though the actual 'working out' of the project was far messier. Such a situation becomes exacerbated when issues of perception are thematic to the work; for acts of perception become inextricably mixed with their representations. The clearest way out of this impasse is to focus not on representation and issues of meaning but on the organisation of the work and its effects. In this regard, the material organisation can be liberated from the meaning and intentionalities that might have prompted it; the work thus will always engender more meaning and find more unanticipated uses than is predicted within the confines of the concept. This is not to imply that all proposals are equivalent, rather that, except for the most limited and extreme circumstances, a necessarily loose fit exists between form and use-form and meaning. Indeed, such correspondences might foster a series of possible uses rather than define any one.

The ancient and perhaps questionable analogy between forms of architecture and forms of music, finds its most recent formulation here in the necessarily loose fit between programme and form. Loose fit of course involves a spectrum of congruencies ranging from the tight fit of the rhyming lyric to the loose fit of the dissonant lyric. In both cases, however, contingency is a fundamental condition as the rhyming or lack of rhyming is not attached in any meaningful way to architectural form.

ORNAMENT AND CONFORMITY

Prominent among the dualisms that have regulated Western architectural thought has been the opposition between ornament and structure. Certainly, within the tendencies which may be associated with modernism that opposition has reached a critical and, one may say, even apocalyptic state; the most radical formulations attempting to erase one of the terms of the opposition (ornament), with the consequent movement of ornament into a covert or recessive condition within the prevailing structure. Postmodern practice, especially the historicist branch, promised to resuscitate ornament in response to what was perceived to be the sterility of a homogenous modernism. Both aspects of the classical relationship, however, continue to be upheld: the oppositional and the hierarchic domination of structure over ornament. On the one hand, ornament is detached from structure as a form of pastiche signage, and on the other, it manifests itself in the adornment of known types, especially in the collagist application of postmodern plan forms.

New architectural potential arises out of a fundamental reappraisal of the status of ornament and its implications for architectural organisation. Axiomatic is the critique, and ultimately, the dismantling of the dualistic structure that has heretofore regulated these conceptions. First and foremost, it should be assumed, contrary to the classical formulation, that ornament is not subservient to structure, but that in fact, ornament is pre-eminently structure in itself; and furthermore, that what would classically be understood as structure is an inherent subset to, and of, the general ornamental organisation. This collapsing of the duality has potentially far-reaching architectural consequences – though not, as one might immediately suppose, as a vehicle for producing yet another ornamentalised architecture. Rather, it employs the ornamental as a graphic instrument capable of engendering complex organisations and spatialities; in other words, those that would foster unforeseen irruptions of institutional forms and programmes.

FROM TYPE TO SCHEMA

Ever since Jean-Nicholas-Louis Durand's 'revolutionary' codification of formal types in his *Recueil* of 1801,[3] architects of varied persuasions have been compelled to position themselves in relation to 'the catalogue'. At stake are issues still hotly contested today: Is it possible (or valuable) to exhaustively roster all that might legitimately fall within the compass of architecture? What is the relationship between the formal and the political? (Not simply the variable relation between a particular form and a particular political doctrine, but perhaps more importantly the assumed apoliticality of typology itself.)

Divergent ideologies have sought to answer these questions within their own monolithic structures. Critical and conservative agendas alike espouse a faith in a universal catalogue of formal types; these are undergirded by the Platonic assumption of the existence of trans-historical models – static and hieratic, and as yet uninfected by the particular accidents of site, programme, materials and politics. (It is, of course, in their particular employments that the ideologies differ.) Novelty, if such a word can be used in this context, would be reserved only for the advent of new type, as for example the railroad terminal or the airport, which would then be added to the 'universal' list. There must be a different apprehension of type by multiplying its conventional limits; or put another way, by encouraging a fundamental shift from type understood as the essential, static geometric lineament underlying building to type as a performative condition: a convergence of flows of graduated scales and limits – to which an inscription of type in the conventional sense represents but an artifact in a field in flux. Complexity theory provides a compelling model (and term) for this shift.

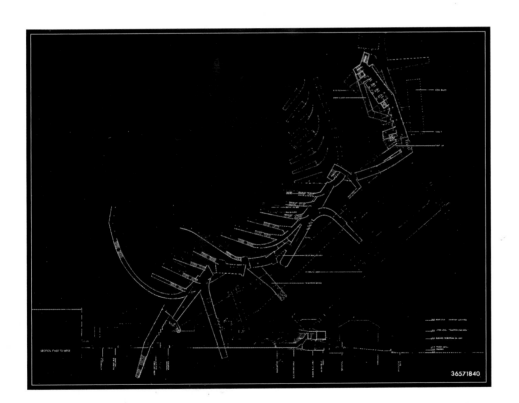

1   Paul Valéry, two fragments from 'The Intellectual Crisis', in *Selected Writings of Paul Valéry*, New Directions Publishing Corporation (New York), 1964, p118.

2   Stan Allen, 'Its Exercise Under Certain Conditions' in *Columbia Documents of Architecture*, vol 13, Columbia University Graduate School of Architecture, Preservation and Planning, 1993, p95.

3   JNL Durand, *Recueil et parallèle des édifices de tout genre, anciens et modernes*, Paris, 1801.

Venice Gateway,
model (top), plan (bottom)

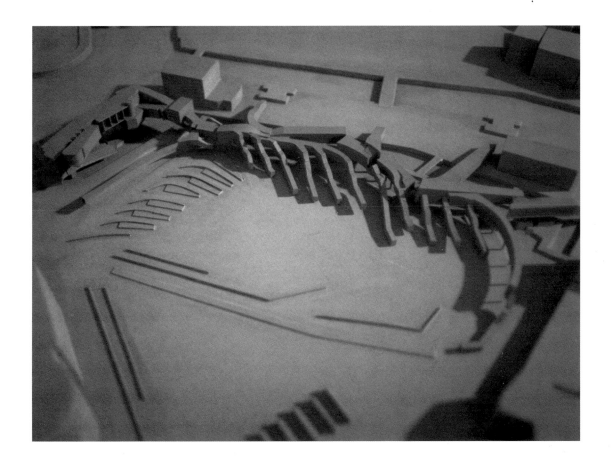

VENICE GATEWAY, 1990, competition entry
for Venice Biennale (with Stan Allen):
aerial view of infrastructural manifold
at Piazzale Roma (left)
model of infrastructural manifold (top)

J JADOW RESIDENCE, MILLRIVER, MASS, 1991, landscape elements: swing/bench, double-cantilevered pergola, supple fence system, and retaining walls (both pages)

BOROS RESIDENCE, SANDS POINT, NEW YORK, 1992,
landscape elements: elevated stone terrace, pump equipment
enclosure/changing room, and canopy structure (both pages)

H JADOW RESIDENCE, MILLRIVER, MASS, 1992:
spa pool of complex topological geometries (opposite)
Co-idle Bridge (above)

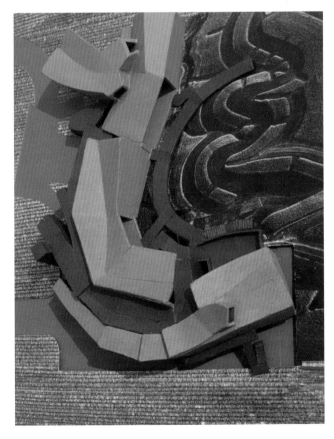

BACHELOR'S APARTMENT, NEW YORK CITY, 1993:
Wing Table (opposite, top)
desk/headboard (opposite, bottom left)
Trough Table (opposite, bottom right)

HEAD START PRE-SCHOOL, EAST WINDSOR, NEW
JERSEY, 1994, competition entry:
views of model (this page)

SPENCE CENTER FOR WOMEN'S HEALTH,
BETHESDA, MA, 1997 (with Debora K Reiser):
views of reception area (both pages)

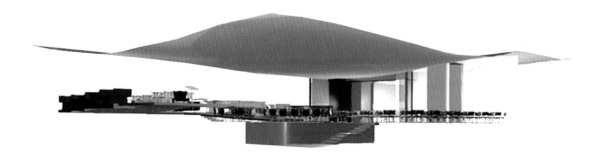

THE BRASSERIE RESTAURANT, SEAGRAM
BUILDING, NEW YORK CITY, 1997, proposal
for a 'relaxed Miesian envelope':
perspectival elevations (top and middle)
ceiling topology (bottom)

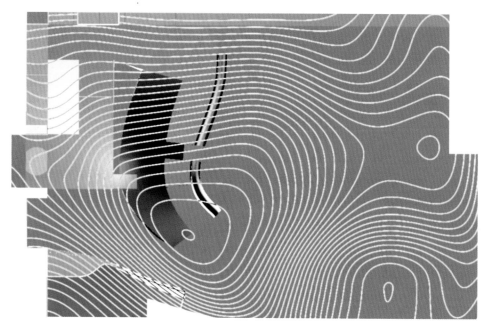

THE BRASSERIE RESTAURANT, SEAGRAM
BUILDING, NEW YORK CITY, 1997:
interior perspectives (above, below)

SOLID-STATE ARCHITECTURE

Jesse Reiser

Here, Reiser + Umemoto respond to the challenges of current architectural debates concerning information technologies and virtual space, which have often rendered the design of buildings a 'dead husk', with a conception of a solid-state architecture. For the partnership, the radical separation that has developed between the virtual and the material found in conventional architectural practice and discourse is seen to have overlooked a fundamental condition of material reality: that of the deeply informative interpenetration of the virtual within the material.

The recent emergence of media-based architecture and the categorical accommodations that have ensued between building-based practices on the one hand, and those which locate architecture in the electronic realm on the other, have paradoxically overlooked a realm of endeavour which actively incorporates one in the other.

The arguments that have been attached to media and its relation to architecture have generally focused on the information technologies associated with electronic or mass-media formations, hence the proliferation of projects by architects that attempt to recover for architectural space the fugitive and placeless condition inherent in electronic technologies. These projects generally assume two forms.

The first approach, which is the more radical of the two, would shift architecture entirely out of the material realm and understand it as a set of orders of protocols, proper and sufficient to themselves. This assumption follows from the position that the advent and implementation of these new technologies renders the forms of order associated with material building obsolete; built architecture in its capacity to enact constraining frameworks (panopticism, disciplinary regimes, etc) has been superseded by virtualised and less tractable forms of control. In the light of this polemic, architecture would be understood as a dead husk that has given up its instrumental ghost, the ghost being set free to proliferate without the material constraints inherent in older architectural formations. Curiously, this approach both reduces architecture to a discipline of control systems while at the same time positing the advent of immaterial architecture as a new-found freedom.

The second more conciliatory approach, exemplified in Jean Nouvel's Bibliothèque Nationale, recognises the continued relevance of building, but conceptually and literally articulates media from building. In this attenuated form of modernism, the place of media assumes a sublimated or classically decorative position within the enframing operation of the building. Electronic media projected on screens or walls updates the fugitive effects (transparency, reflectivity, etc) found in earlier modernisms. What remains constant, however, is the classical hierarchy governing the relationship between structure and ornament, with literal structure forming a limiting and regulating framework within which media/ornament might be domesticated.

Ultimately, these models derive from a history that would first locate the effective means of power in architecture as being coextensive with building up to the end of the classical period and would then trace the progressive liberation of those power structures – ultimately in the media – from their material constraints. Thus, from the viewpoint of architecture as a power structure, its material form becomes increasingly ineffective, hence a loss of architecture/power as material manifestation and the consequent migration of architecture/power to the electronic realm. While this logic might be historically visible, it does not follow that it is the only logic or the most productive way of operating as an architect who sees a continued relevance in material constructs.

Switchback road – a primary complexity

A vital distinction was made by the French philosopher Gilles Deleuze in relation to the modalities and uses of power in his comparison between Foucault's term *pouvoir* and Nietzsche's *puissance*. Both are usually translated as 'power', but Nietzsche's *puissance* is the power to act – potential – while *pouvoir* is the codified image of such 'active' power in reactive 'powers that be', which define and constrain what is possible. *Puissance* opens up possibilities and capacities, while *pouvoir* closes them off, regimenting passive subjects by defining their roles or formal 'capacities'.[1] I would hazard to suggest that the degree to which the aforementioned models of architectural practice prioritise representational space, whether by process or critique, passively abets the totalising forces outlined by Foucault.

Any work of architecture may be discussed in terms of what it is or what it signifies. The crucial question here, especially in relation to design practice, is the effect that such conceptions have on the formation and ultimately on the performance of the architecture itself. Signification as a by-product or effect is both as inevitable as it is changeable. The kind of determinations it brings to a work, both in terms of process and product, stand in opposition to an architecture of becoming. *Puissance* suggests a fundamental shift away from power as a representational form to that of an active principle, and in respect to architecture this would mean 'taking the actual flow in historical conditions as its privileged materiality'.[2]

I would like to outline a third approach which builds on the idea of *puissance*. In doing so, it would be important to shift the sense and the way media is understood in an architectural context. This entails a rather untimely mixing of traditional architectural practices with emerging notions of complexity. What this means is emphasising the building's economy and thus its activity as a building. Consequently, instead of viewing the building in terms of representation or symbolisation, what is at stake is its own internal economy. Change thus becomes an active expression of the material organisation of the building.

In claiming that the first two models of media in architecture engage too narrow a band width, we are neither calling for a repudiation of these practices nor positioning ourselves in some dialectical relationship to them, but rather are recognising that they fail to engage notions of media that are inherent in architecture as a material process and practice. As Deleuze writes in the article curiously enough entitled 'Mediators':

> Philosophy, art, and science come into relations of mutual resonance and exchange, but always for internal reasons. The way in which they impinge on one another depends on their own evolution. A discipline that set out to follow a creative movement coming from outside would itself relinquish any creative role. You'll get nowhere by latching onto some parallel movement, you have to make a move yourself. If nobody makes a move, nobody gets anywhere. Nor is it interplay and exchange: it all turns on giving or taking.[3]

While mass media directs flows of disembodied information, we will move laterally along the electromagnetic spectrum and emphasise a materially engaged notion of media, and following from that, media's informative capacities in relation to built architectural space. I would like to characterise this new form of practice as operating in the so-called 'solid state'.

I choose the term because the notion of solid state carries with it the idea that material formations are inextricably linked to the computational logics inherent in materiality itself, what Sanford Kwinter calls 'wet computation'. Therefore, in contrast to the two models outlined earlier, the heavy recalcitrant and inert condition of building need not be divorced from virtualities. This solid-state notion of architecture, then, will engage media in two distinct yet related ways: the first, media as a material substance (like a painter's medium); and the second, media as a virtual or informing potential. These are not, in practice, separate notions or procedures, but rather can be said to be folded together within the conception of the diagram.

As architects we are apt to regard diagramming in terms of either the fixed norms of classical geometry and typology or as reductive descriptions of programmatic or functional relations (bubble diagramming). If, however, we shift our focus from such static models

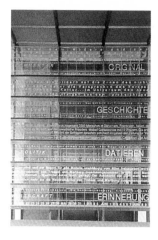

Bibliothèque Nationale, Paris,
Jean Nouvel (top)
Virtual Architecture,
Stephen Perrella (bottom)

to dynamical (essentially time-based) systems then an entirely new horizon of possibilities emerges. 'Time in other words, reappears in the world as something real, as a destabilizing but creative milieu'.[4] A corresponding shift, therefore, is necessary from the fixed, bounded geometry of classicism to a language of waves, fields and fronts. (Incidentally, the fundamental breakthrough in solid-state physics came about in the shift from grids to lattices.) Along with this shift come distinctly unclassical notions of universality. Temporal/material fluxes, what Manuel de Landa calls 'figures of destiny', are singular incarnations of order whose lineaments come into being momentarily;[5] as such they are not distant, prior to, or above the material conditions that spawned them. An even more disquieting, yet eminently useful, universal structure emerges: that is of the dynamical diagram, which has no essential origin, and can be incarnated in multiple materials, scales and regimes. The use value of the diagram lies not in a capacity for representation, but rather in its latent potential for quantitative effects. Initially, the diagram carries a kind of proportionality which ultimately locks into a specific order, material and scale. This describes a particular and local necessity, a solid state, wrought from an initially variable diagram. For architects, this means that the nonlinear dynamics found, for example, in weather systems are already at the level of order, possible to instrumentalise architecturally with the stuff inherent in architecture; neither metaphor nor symbol, but a literal employment of the order itself.

Von Karman vortices formed by islands

These issues will be further elaborated through a discussion of a recent project for a water garden for Jeffrey Kipnis. Just as the upward thrust of a mountain range breaks up the orderly flow of winds around the earth surface, creating local eddies which in turn affect temperature and rainfall, so the variegated peaks and valleys of the water garden exert a spectrum of turbulent effects on the flow space of the garden; and like the relative fixity of the mountain range (whose movement could only be mapped in geological time) versus the rapidity of the weather, the time, materials and forces involved in the strata of the garden embody radically different times of formation versus the times of effect. Indeed, while the 'origins' of the diagrams that determine the three strata of the garden could not be more disparate, their exchanges are not. The meaning of the relationship among them arises not in their origins but in the way the diagrams communicate through their material incarnations. While history is not communicated, force is. The magnitude and directions of a force, its vectorial resultant, finds expression not simply in itself, but non-linearly in the adjoining media. These exchanges, while mutual, are not equal. The dominant media (in this case the fixed geometry of the slab) exerts proportionally greater influence than the relatively weak forces of the flow space. This is not a simple dominance, however. Lateral efflorescences, mineral and vegetal, engender moving tracks that criss-cross the flow space, dissipating the determinations of the slab. In addition, the fine-scaled effects of surface tension and meniscus are amplified by the ogive geometry of the grooves. Every change in water level results in a new and changing constellation of puddles and walking surfaces. Such effects are accelerated as the water rises because the geometry of the ogive tends increasingly towards the horizontal with every increase in the vertical dimension.

One can carry the weather analogy further: that the same mountain range, and indeed the same air flow can produce a multitude of local weather effects from fogs to thunderstorms. This can be accounted for by the fact that the air is not a uniform media but is widely variable in terms of temperature and humidity, which in turn determines its stability or instability. Interaction with the mountain range triggers the release of potentials latent in the air mass, thus the same mountain range will trigger fogs in stable air mass and thunderstorms in the unstable one.

An issue associated with this notion of material mediation is the role of geometry, specifically topological geometries. Distinct from classical Euclidean geometry, these geometries develop potentials to engage flows in living and non-living systems. And here it is important to clarify that this media-form relationship is not understood metaphorically or symbolically but as a direct instrumentality with the capability of producing architectural effects.[6]

Notions of inside–outside, figure–ground, centre–periphery – in short the entire repertoire of spatial models attached to classical geometry – have come to be reformulated not so much as an overturning of these models, but as a complexification. As architects, we employ mathematical constructs in necessarily impure form, therefore the contingencies that are inherent in architecture (site, scale, programme, structure, etc) become mixed with the so-called pure mathematics. This does not mean architecture is merely a corrupt form of mathematics but rather:

> There are notions that are exact in nature, quantitative, defined by equations, and whose very meaning lies in their exactness: an architect can use these only metaphorically and that's quite wrong, because they belong to exact science but there are also essentially inexact yet completely rigorous notions that scientists can't do without, which belong equally to scientists, philosophers, and architects.[7]

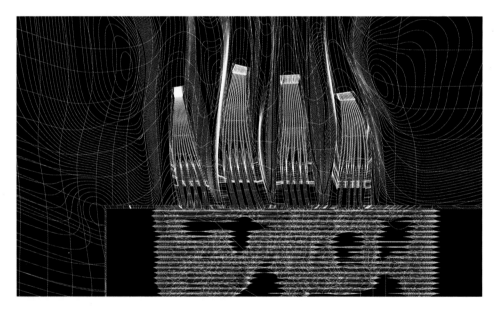

Water Gardens, topographic study

1   Gilles Deleuze, *Negotiations: 1972–1990*, Columbia University Press (New York), 1995, p199.

2   Sanford Kwinter, 'Flying the Bullet, Or Where the Future Began', pre-publication manuscript, p1.

3   Gilles Deleuze, 'Mediators', *Negotiations: 1972–1990*, Columbia University Press (New York), 1995, p125.

4   Sanford Kwinter, 'Landscapes of Change: Boccioni's Stati D'Animo as a General Theory of Models', in *Assemblage 19*, MIT Press (Cambridge, Mass), 1992, p52.

5   Manuel de Landa, 'Nonorganic Life' in *Zone 6: 1 Incorporations*, Zone Books, MIT Press (Cambridge, Mass), 1993.

6   This conception of architecture's effective capacities is derived from Jeff Kipnis' article in 'Towards a New Architecture' in 'Folding in Architecture', *Architectural Design* Profile no 102, Academy Editions (London), February 1993, pp40-9.

7   Gilles Deleuze, 'On a Thousand Plateaus' from *Negotiations: 1972–1990*, Columbia University Press (New York), 1995, p29. The term 'architects' has been inserted into Deleuze's text by Reiser.

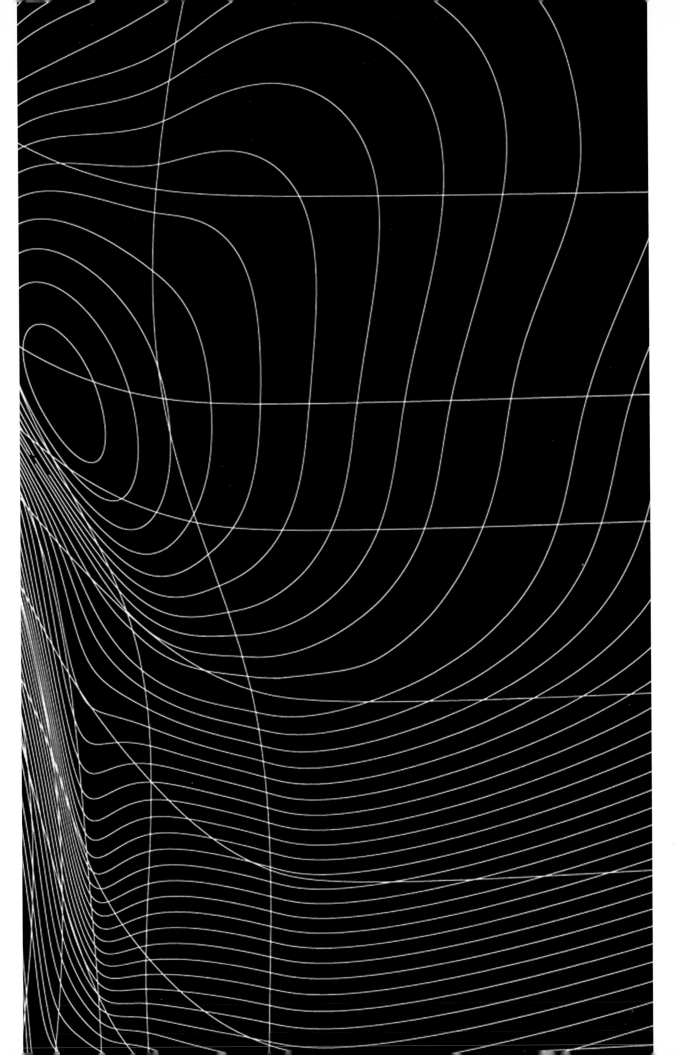

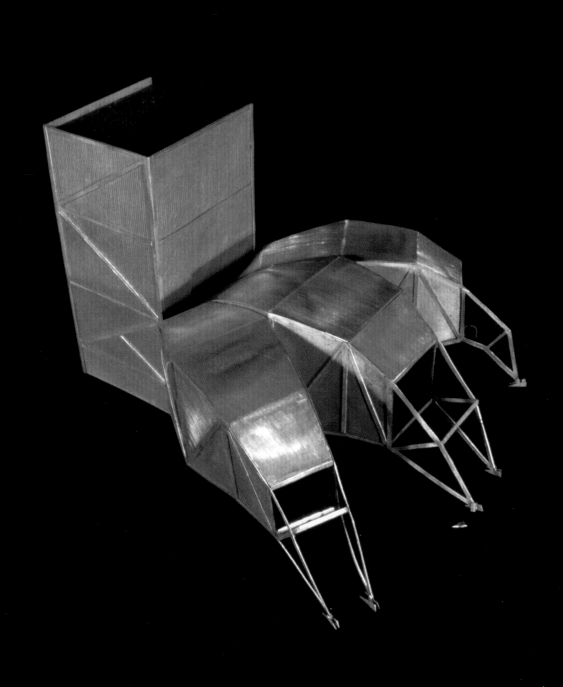

CARDIFF BAY OPERA HOUSE, WALES

Competition Entry, 1994

SOME NOTES ON GEODETICS

We view our Cardiff Bay Opera House proposal as a test-bed for the speculative use of geodetics. This system's geometric, structural, material and organisational implications have historically been subjected to narrow interpretation due to the ideological climate of early modernism. With the dissolution of modernist notions of ideality comes the opportunity to re-employ systems of order in broader and less constrained terms. Our interest lies not in a revisionist history, but rather in the immediate and expanded efficacy that systems such as geodetics offer. We would note that our use of geodetics is a tactical one: only the foyer/concourse – the difficult zone of transition from the scale of the urban to the scale of the auditorium seat – is negotiated fluidly using the continuous logic of geodetics.

The current discussion regarding the tactics of achieving formal and programmatic heterogeneity in the realm of architecture and planning has occasioned a reassessment of spatial models and technologies previously relegated to the scrapheap of utopian modernism. Such modernist systems have come to be associated with the structures of a totalising spatial ideology and an attempt to produce homogeneous and unified architectural languages.[1] Among these discarded or relegated technologies stands the geometric and structural conception known as geodesics or geodetics.[2] Popularised by Buckminster Fuller and his followers as an architectural and urbanistic panacea, they are presently encountered in the occasional fairground structure or military installation (usually in the form of a dome). Fuller's geodesics have been detached from the utopian projections. But this history has unfortunately obscured a prior and, ironically, more open set of possibilities in the field of descriptive morphology and aeronautics.

The structural system known as geodetics, developed by the English engineer Sir Barnes Wallis, was first used in the R-100 Airship and later in the Vickers Wellesley; its most famous employment was as the structure of the Wellington Bomber. Geodetics derives from the Greek term *geodesis*, the imaginary geographical lines following the curvature of the earth along straight paths. The property of a geodetic system is to carry all loads along the shortest possible paths, hence producing a criss-cross pattern of self-stabilising members by means of which loads in any direction are automatically equalised by forces in the intersecting set of frames. This results in a structure that is extremely light and strong.[3] Its durability is due, in part, to the inherent characteristic of extreme redundancy: if some portion of the structure is lost, the stresses are simply rerouted to the remaining members. Therefore, one can say that in distinction to most conventional spatial-structural systems, geodetics is structurally diffuse or nonessential.

A contemporary of Barnes Wallis (and possibly an influence) was the biologist D'Arcy Wentworth Thompson from whose book, *On Growth and Form*, comes the following:

> If we take any two points on a smooth curved surface, such as that of a sphere or spheroid, and imagine a string stretched between them, we obtain what is known in mathematics as a geodetic curve. It is the shortest line which can be traced between the two points upon the surface itself, and it has always the same direction upon the surface to which it is confined; the most familiar of all cases, from which the name is derived, is that curve or 'rhumb line' upon the earth's surface which the navigator learns to follow in the practice of 'great circle sailing,' never altering his direction nor departing from his nearest road. Where the surface is spherical, the geodesic is literally a great circle, a circle, that is to say, whose center is the center of the sphere. If instead of a sphere we are dealing with a spheroid,

auditorium claw – flight space (opposite)
fuselages of Wellington Bombers under
construction at Vickers factory (top)

whether prelate or oblate (that is to say, a figure of revolution in which an ellipse rotates about its long or its short axis), then the system of geodesics becomes more complicated. For in it the elliptic meridians are all geodesics, and so is the circle of the equator; though the circles of latitude are not so, any more than in the sphere. But a line which crosses the equator at an oblique angle, if it is to be geodesic, will go on so far and then turn back again, winding its way in a continual figure-of-eight curve between two extreme latitudes, as when we wind a ball of wool. To say, as we have done, that the geodesic is the shortest line between two points upon the surface, is as much to say that it is a *trace* of some particular straight line upon the surface in question, and it follows that, if any linear body be confined to that surface, while retaining a tendency to grow (save only for its confinement to that surface) in a straight line, the resultant form which it will assume will be that of a geodesic.[4]

As an aviation technology, geodetics represents something of an anomaly, a short-lived tributary from the mainstream technology that tended increasingly towards stressed-skin construction. Though geodetics was a versatile system that could conform to the intricacies of aircraft configuration, it was typically cost prohibitive due to its inherent complexity. In effect, each aircraft became a highly crafted object that required special dies and hand-bending jigs for each strut.[5]

In an architectural context, however, with the interest in structural systems that could engender complexity through flexibility, geodetics becomes interesting precisely because, as a system, it is capable of adapting to complex spatial formations without a corresponding increase in the complexity of the system. In geodetics exact geometries such as the dome are no more ideal than any number of other volumetric configurations. Moreover, the advent of computer-linked design and fabrication has obviated the technical difficulties encountered in earlier employments.

In a 'supple' employment of geodetics one finds many properties and possibilities. Historically and operationally, geodetics falls between two totalising systems, the skeletal model – structure and skin – and the structural skin model as a monocoque construction.[6] On a possible expanded reading, however, geodetics acts as a structural tissue or flesh – an intermediate structure that would assemble heterogeneous agglomerations of space, programme and path. Moreover, geodetics is protean in the sense that the structure has the capability of changing and adapting to the space that it develops in a number of ways: by changing the fineness or coarseness of its reticulations; by growing or multiplying the number of struts or crossovers; by mimicking the surfaces of, for example, conventional structures into or on to which it is projected; or by changing by degrees the type of infill or skinning that it carries. Our Cardiff Bay Opera House project explores some of these architectural implications of geodetics.

CARDIFF BAY OPERA HOUSE
This project seeks to involve the opera house in the unique historical and spatial configuration of Cardiff's inner harbour area by constituting the project as a series of infrastructural events. The nature and limits of the house are redefined at both extremes of its scale: as an integral part of the city and its environs, and as a setting for a stage performance. The building, therefore, is not understood as an isolated monument but as an open cultural form that is capable of meeting imperatives and needs like the docks, tunnels and roads that structure the harbour itself.

CIRCULATION
The opera house site is organised according to three distinct patterns of pedestrian and vehicular access. Firstly, pedestrian access from the oval piazza occurs on an incline by way of direct entry into the concourse. Secondly, car and taxi access is kept distinct from pedestrian passage by linking Pierhead Street at the south-east side of the site with James Street at the north-west, creating a vehicular court through the centre of the site that allows for ample covered drop-off and waiting space along the inside face of the concourse; access to underground parking is also from the vehicular court. Thirdly, the delivery of scenery and other large objects by heavy goods vehicles is made by way of a one-way elevated service road, entering from Pierhead Street, ramping up and following the northern edge of the site and ramping down to exit at James Street.

Cardiff Bay Opera House,
infrastructural routes

THE CONCOURSE/FOYER

The concourse/foyer element is the crucial link between the exterior public spaces and the events in the opera house complex. To this end, a form is proposed that would maximise transparency and exchange between the piazza and concourse at ground level and between the auditorium and foyers above. This 'geodetic bag' of the concourse/foyer divides into three tubes, which then insinuate themselves into the respective prongs of the theatre 'claw'. These insinuations develop the lobby forms for the auditorium. Their meandering plan form enables a total continuity between foyer and auditorium that blocks sound and light transmission between the spaces. No doors are necessary. While extensively glazed on the exposed exterior surfaces, the 'bag' changes its surfacing material in contact with the auditorium volume to become the acoustical lining of lobbies and the auditorium proper.

THE AUDITORIUM

The auditorium comprises three bridges joined at one end spanning the space between the stage/flytower volume and the foyer/concourse. The form of the auditorium is created out of the desire to combine the advantages of intimacy and early lateral sound reflections, as provided in the traditional shoe-box hall, with the significantly larger seating requirements of the competition brief. To achieve this, the three shoe-box halls are notionally joined together and each splayed on angles. Two large prows are left at the joints to provide a large, sound-reflective side-wall area for the rear seats, where the side walls of the three halls merge and disappear. The necessary lateral reflection to the central seats is provided by segmenting the main floor into three areas, with the second-level seating rising above the first-level seating. The steps between the two levels form a vertical sound reflecting surface that provides early lateral sound energy to the seats on the first level.

WELSH NATIONAL OPERA REHEARSAL FACILITIES

The rehearsal facilities are designed for the possibility of simultaneous 'in-house' and public performance. The configuration of four rehearsal spaces is inherently flexible. It allows them to be used independently, in conjunction with one another, or as a single large space. A steel-roller-blind curtain system creates the necessary movable partitions. The entire floor area is divided into eighty platforms. These can be moved hydraulically, making the topography of the floor infinitely variable and thus achieving virtually any form of theatrical arrangement of stage, platform, apron, seating rake, tower or terrain.

Cardiff Bay Opera House, site plan

1   Greg Lynn, 'Architectural Curvilinearity: The Folded, the Pliant and the Supple', 'Folding in Architecture', *Architectural Design* (London), no 102, 1993, pp8-15.

2   The terms 'geodetic' and 'geodesic' are technically interchangeable; we will distinguish the 'supple' employment from the modernist one (like Buckminster Fuller's) by letting Barnes Wallis' term, geodetics, stand for the former.

3   William Green, *Famous Bombers of the Second World War*, vol 1, MacDonald Press (London), 1959.

4   D'Arcy Wentworth Thompson, *On Growth and Form*, Dover (New York), 1992, pp675-76.

5   Martin Bowman, *Wellington, the Geodetic Giant Airlife* (Shrewsbury), 1989, pp3-5.

6   Monocoque, from Greek *monos* and French *coque*, meaning 'single shell'. In the pure monocoque structure, there is no external bracing; the shell bears all the load. A semimonocoque design, which has stiffeners running the length of the fuselage, is also referred to by engineers as a stressed-skin construction.

CARDIFF BAY OPERA HOUSE:
aerial view of complex (opposite, top)
view of site (opposite, bottom)
night view from oval basin (above)

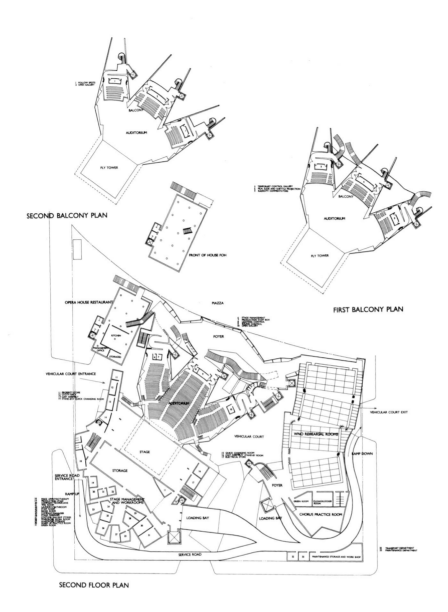

SECOND BALCONY PLAN

FIRST BALCONY PLAN

SECOND FLOOR PLAN

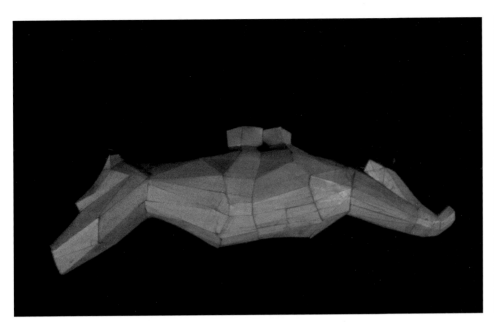

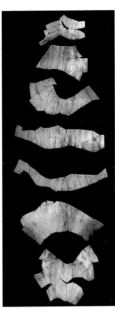

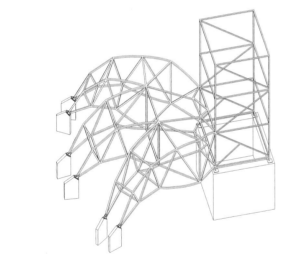

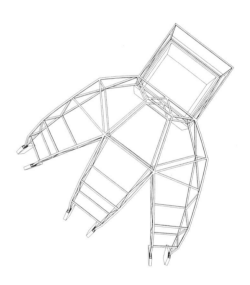

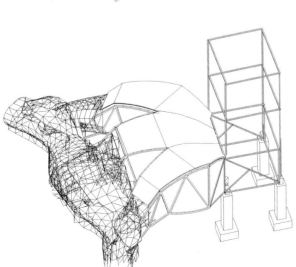

CARDIFF BAY OPERA HOUSE:
floor plans (opposite top)
longitudinal section (opposite bottom)

geodetic bag (top left)
geodetic pattern (top right)
structural drawings (above)

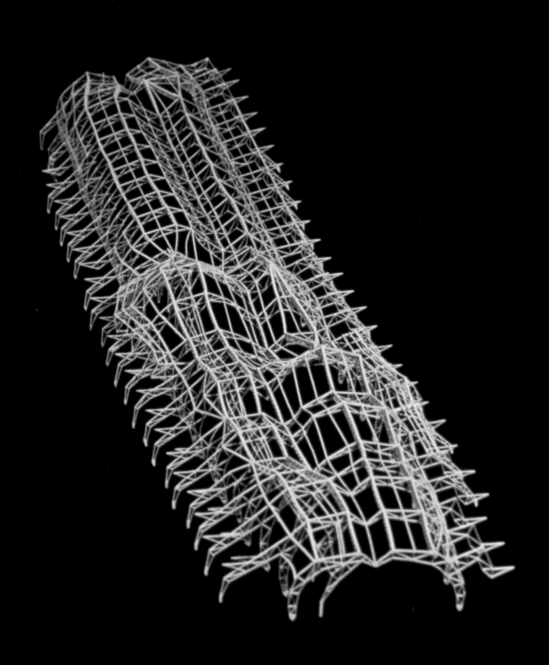

YOKOHAMA PORT TERMINAL, JAPAN

Competition Entry, 1995

CONCEPT

The starting point for this proposal was the inherent duality between global systems of transport and exchange and the condition of the specific sites upon which such systems cross. Situated in central Japan on Tokyo Bay, the port of Yokohama, and even more specifically its terminal, exemplifies this duality. The proposal responds to this by encompassing the general functional imperatives of the cruise terminal, as a smoothly functioning link between land and water transport, and the specific civic possibilities suggested by the pier configuration itself.

The terminal is conceived as an incomplete or partial building – partial, both conceptually and formally, in recognition of the fact that such programmes frame thresholds in two distinct yet overlapping continuums: in the cycle of embarkation and disembarkation of cruise ships; and at the civic level as a place of rest and recreation in the course of an excursion. Consequently, completion, both physically and virtually, is effected only periodically: in the linkage of terminal to cruise ship or in the closure of the completed urban event.

THE STRUCTURE

The proposed terminal is a shed building measuring 412 metres (1,352 feet) in length, comprising twenty-seven, three-hinged, steel-trussed arches of 42.5 metres (139 feet) average span placed at 16-metre (52.5 feet) intervals. These arches are joined longitudinally by trussed members of conventional configuration and purling, carrying either metal cladding or the extensive glazing envisioned for the project. The steel-shed structure springs from hinges placed at the surface of the main level. These are carried on concrete piers extending from the basement-parking level through the apron to the surface of the main level. Horizontal thrust from the arches is counteracted by tension rods connecting opposing arch hinges. These tension rods also serve as partial support for the main-floor slab.

This large shed, though affiliated with its nineteenth-century antecedents, differs in the sense that while large-scale structures of the previous century were characterised by a totalising conception employing uniform and repetitive structural units enclosing a single homogeneous space, this proposal engenders heterogeneity through selective perturbations and extensions of the structural frames. This transformation yields a complex of spaces, smoothly incorporating the multiple terminal, civic and garden schemes within and below its span.

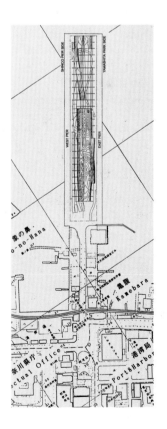

VEHICULAR CIRCULATION

Vehicular access into the port terminal is effected by either one of two routes. The first is a ramped dual roadway accessed from the root of the pier, rising 18 metres (59 feet) above ground level. Traversing the length of the major programmatic elements of the terminal along their periphery, it terminates in the loop of the traffic plaza. This route enables one to pass through the trussed out riggers of the arches while experiencing an unfolding view from the Shinco side of the pier.

The traffic plaza meets both the needs of the cruise terminal and the public – providing direct access into the departures and arrivals hall as well as ramp access to underground parking. The second means of egress is a two-lane access road, which descends from the pier root to an underground car park for 600 cars. The departures and arrivals hall and public facilities above are entered by banks of elevators.

structural frame (opposite)
site model (top)
site plan (bottom)

THE PROGRAMME

The main level, which is 5 metres (16.4 feet) above ground, is comprised of the principal spaces related to cruise ship embarkation and disembarkation. They are disposed in a linear symmetric composition along the longitudinal axis of the pier. From the traffic plaza curbside drop-off, one may enter directly in the departures and arrivals hall. This hall leads directly into the Customs/Immigration/Quarantine (CIQ) facility, as well as providing access to the visitors' deck, public facilities and gardens via two symmetrical staircases and associated elevators. Beyond the CIQ facilities lies the departures and arrivals lobby where the main access to the cruise decks occurs on both the east and west sides of the space. Staircases to the apron are also provided for occasional embarkation and disembarkation from that level. At the top of the pier end of the traffic plaza, access is gained to the cafeteria and restaurant facilities above, as well as to the sea bus below.

The public facilities and gardens occupy the uppermost portions of the terminal shed. Two principal means of access are available to this elevated urban facility – one from a grand exterior stair located at the pier root of the terminus of Kaigandori and the second from extensions of the symmetrical staircases located in the departures and arrivals hall. Corresponding elevators also provide access from these locations. It is also proposed that these facilities would represent a direct extension of the existing urban promenade leading to the pier. They have been designed to be accessible even when the port terminal is not in use.

NIWAMINATO

The concept of Niwaminato, or 'garden-port', was addressed in the formation of the shed as a whole. The competition brief required the coexistence of two distinct urban programmes: a port terminal and a continually accessible public amenity in the form of a garden. Our strategy renders these distinct programmes coextensive yet discretely connected (the operation of the port terminal is predicated on specific zones of access and quarantine).

Its convoluted surface developed to generate a series of urban/landscape effects. These effects manifest themselves in an artificial terrain in the overall configuration and silhouette of the building envelope, and the deployment of a series of interconnected garden programmes and promenades on and within the thickness of this roof terrain. The gardens include: linear promenades along and adjacent to the visitors' deck; exposed deck gardens; vertically negotiable roof terrain; and enclosed year-round greenhouse gardens located within the depth of the arch-roof trusses.

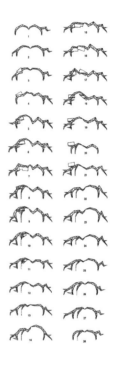

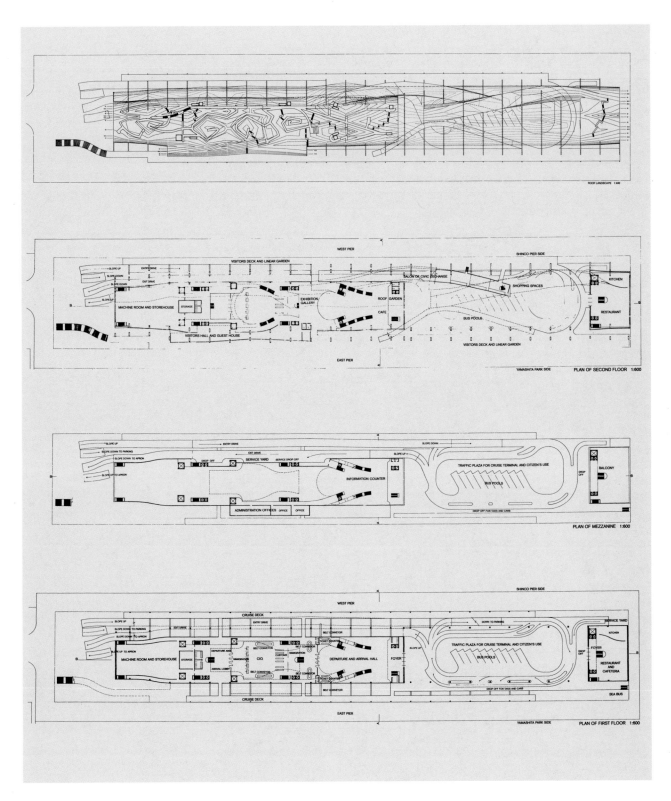

YOKOHAMA PORT TERMINAL:
structural skeleton (opposite top)
structural elevation facing tip of pier and
end structural elevation (opposite bottom)

roof landscape
plan of second floor
plan of mezzanine
plan of first floor

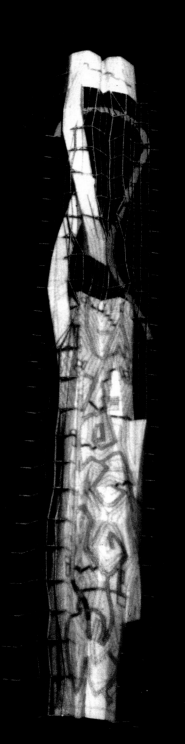
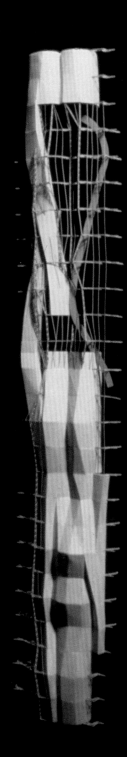
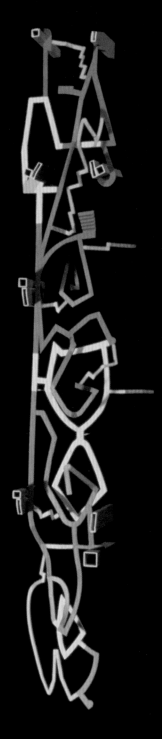

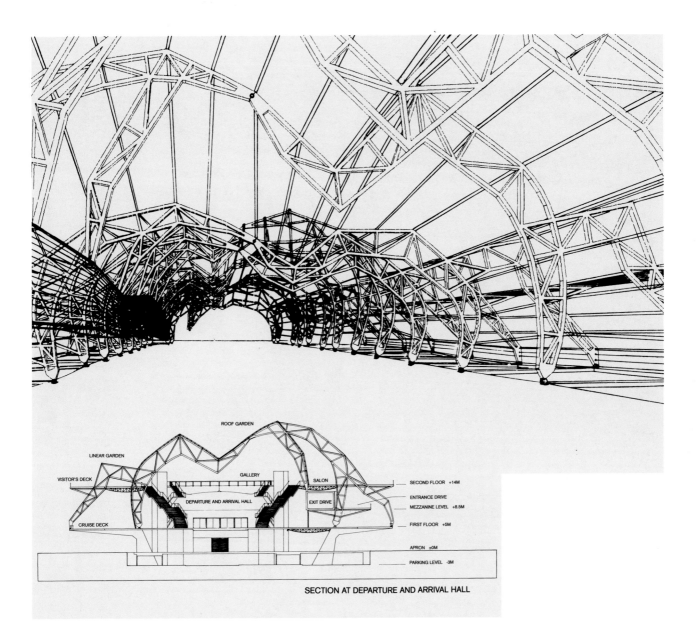

SECTION AT DEPARTURE AND ARRIVAL HALL

ROOF GARDEN

LINEAR GARDEN

VISITOR'S DECK

GALLERY

SALON

DEPARTURE AND ARRIVAL HALL

EXIT DRIVE

CRUISE DECK

SECOND FLOOR +14M

ENTRANCE DRIVE

MEZZANINE LEVEL +8.5M

FIRST FLOOR +5M

APRON ±0M

PARKING LEVEL -3M

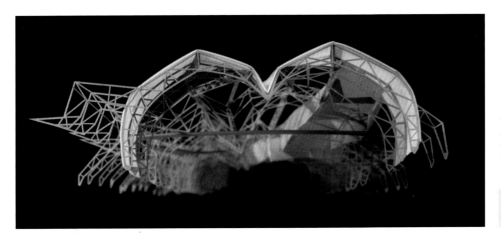

YOKOHAMA PORT TERMINAL:
terminal roof with
terrain/path system (opposite left)
terminal roof (opposite middle)
path system (opposite right)

structural perspective (top)
section (middle)
elevation of pier end (bottom)

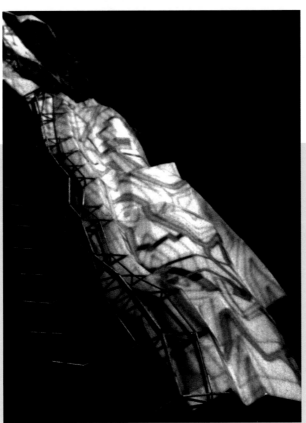

YOKOHAMA PORT TERMINAL:
roof detail (opposite)
underside of terminal roof (top)
roof terrain (bottom)

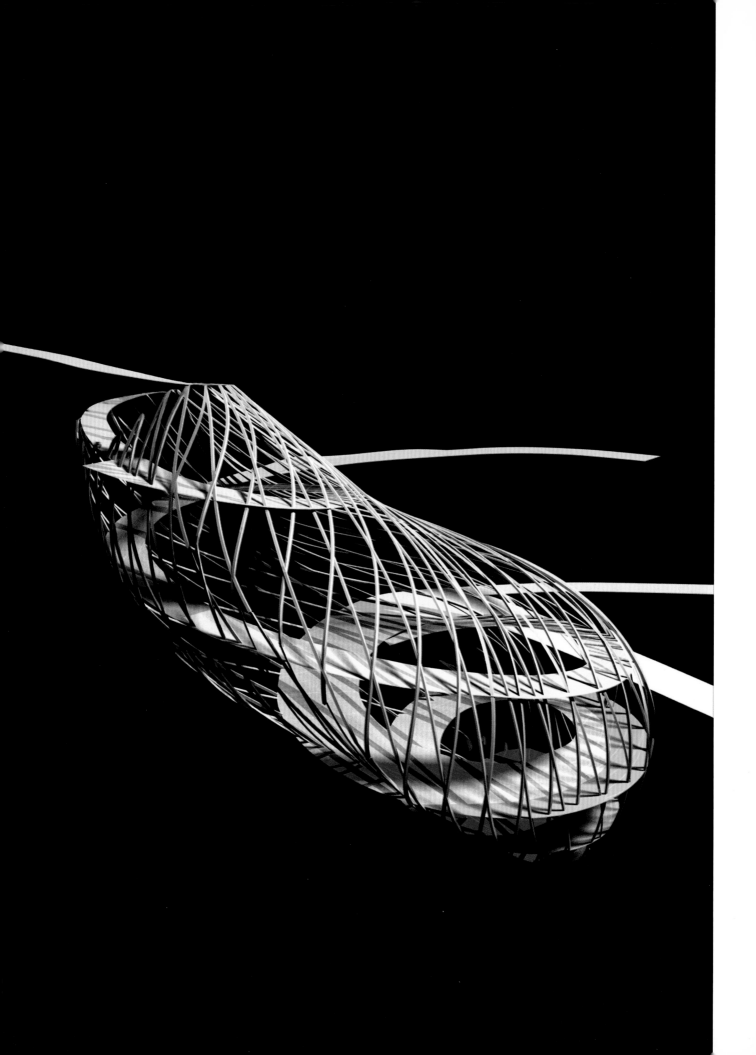

KANSAI LIBRARY, JAPAN
Competition Entry, 1996

The proposal for the Kansai Kan of the National Diet Library addresses the apparent paradox thrown up by the universal proliferation of data, which despite the presumed placelessness of information persistently requires an architectural definition for its condition. Beyond the admittedly important legal and archival necessity for preserving 'hard copies' of documents, the persistence of the library may be ascribed to less recognised processes attendant to globalisation. The general phenomena of decentralisation and dispersion of institutions, made possible by new technologies, overshadow a correspondingly specific trend towards centrality and agglomeration both within and appended to major urban centres in global economies. Japan's principal cities (where most of the country's data is produced and consumed) have seen the advent of information zones: an amassing of buildings and public spaces relatively small in scale whose organisation promotes mutual interests and information exchange through direct communication. A new form of public space thus arises out of the interaction of two logics: first, the close proximity of major institutions and corporations, and second, this consequent influx of smaller institutions and services that are sustained by the presence of their larger neighbours. The success of such co-dependent organisations is predicated not simply by the major institutions that initiate the information zone, but by their capacity to act as catalysts for the advent of new programmes and uses. This proposal, therefore, embodies two distinct yet related imperatives: to fulfil the explicit use of the library, while developing implicit spatialities that would foster new and unforeseen irruptions of programme brought about by the 'information zone'.

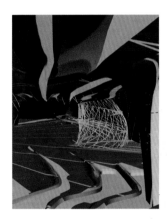

THE STACK BUILDING
The stack building is a bar measuring 182 metres (597.8 feet) in length, 25 metres (82 feet) in width and 25 metres in height. It is comprised of steel-truss walls, oriented vertically, acting as gigantic storage units for automated, compact and fixed stacks. Books and documents are accessed via catwalks and the automated conveyor system, which efficiently routes library materials to and from the reading rooms and Operational System Department for shipping and receiving external deliveries. Since the stack building is organised around the concept of the storage wall, stacks – automated, compact and fixed – are categorised sectionally in layers. There are no horizontal slabs or floors as such in the stack building. Horizontal movement is effected by catwalks and the automated conveyor system. Between the storage walls are narrow open wells from ground to roof, allowing filtered natural illumination to enter the entire section of the building through skylights.

PUBLIC SPACES
The library building, measuring 220 x 55 metres (721.8 x 180.4 feet), is comprised of three ramped slabs suspended by cables from a prestressed-steel roof carried on four steel piers. The slabs are so formed as to maximise continuity and multiple interconnection among the public spaces and levels. Topological deformations – cuts, mounds, ramps, ripples and stairs – render the library a programmed landscape that has the capacity not only to fulfil the smooth functioning of the main scheme, but also to foster the emergence of new and unanticipated configurations of social space. The visitors enter the library from two locations. Visitors arriving on foot and by bus gain access via the pedestrian road located at the front of the building at Seika Main Street; a ramp leads up to the second level and joins the drop-off

geodetic store (opposite)
public library space (above)

point for cars in front of this main entrance. Entry into the lobby is also possible from the parking level via ramps. The lobby space provides a direct entrance into the restaurant, store, lockers and auditorium above. Controlled access into the main reading room is possible through five ramps which lead to the surface of the reading room above. The scheme of the library is based on the notion of precincts rather than dividing walls. Consequently, the main reading room's activities bleed both into the floor below and the Asian Document and Information Center farther up the ramp.

STRUCTURE AND RESISTANCE TO LATERAL FORCES

The library building is comprised of three ramped, two-way, prestressed-concrete slabs 20 centimetres (7.9 inches) thick; the whole of which is suspended from a prestressed-steel roof of 6 metres (19.7 inches) maximum depth by a 9 metre (29.5 feet) grid of suspension cables 5 centimetres (2 inches) in diameter passing through the ramped slabs. The roof is carried on four integral steel piers. The large plan dimension of the slabs and roof necessitates distinct responses to lateral forces: thermal, seismic and wind. Each concrete slab is divided in two across the long dimension by a thermal expansion joint with mechanical dampers to absorb any lateral dynamic movement. The prestressed-steel roof requires no expansion joint: it transmits its relatively large lateral thermal expansion to its four piers, two of which are fixed to footings; the opposing pair being allowed to slide freely on Teflon pads. The perimeter of the entire library building is enclosed by a lattice truss of 20-centimetre (7.9 inch), welded-steel tubes. The ramp/roof assembly thus forms a rigid box enabling resistance to any anticipated lateral earthquake forces. Further, vertical seismic movement is effectively dampened by the relative flexibility of roof and slab assemblies.

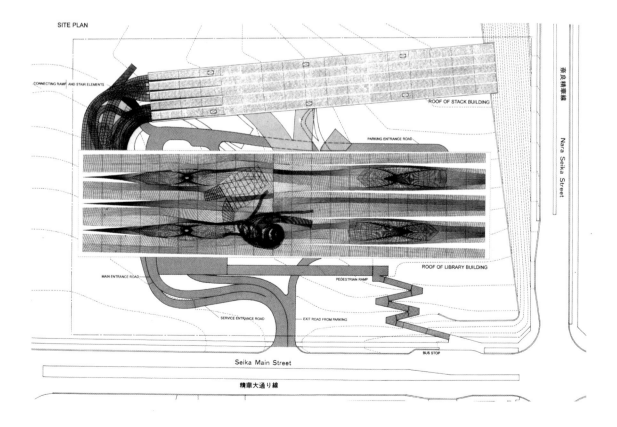

SITE PLAN

CONNECTING RAMP AND STAIR ELEMENTS

ROOF OF STACK BUILDING

PARKING ENTRANCE ROAD

ROOF OF LIBRARY BUILDING

MAIN ENTRANCE ROAD

PEDESTRIAN RAMP

SERVICE ENTRANCE ROAD

EXIT ROAD FROM PARKING

BUS STOP

Nara Seika Street

奈良精華線

Seika Main Street

精華大通り線

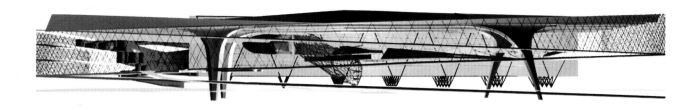

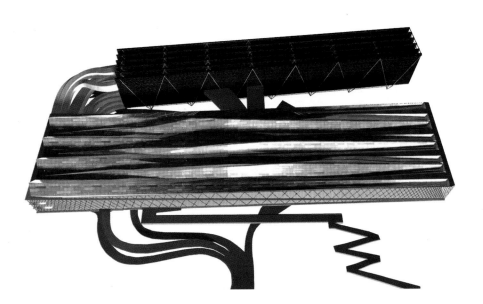

KANSAI LIBRARY:
site plan (opposite)
interior view (top)
west elevation (middle)
aerial perspective (bottom)

topological geometries of roof
and floor plates (overleaf)

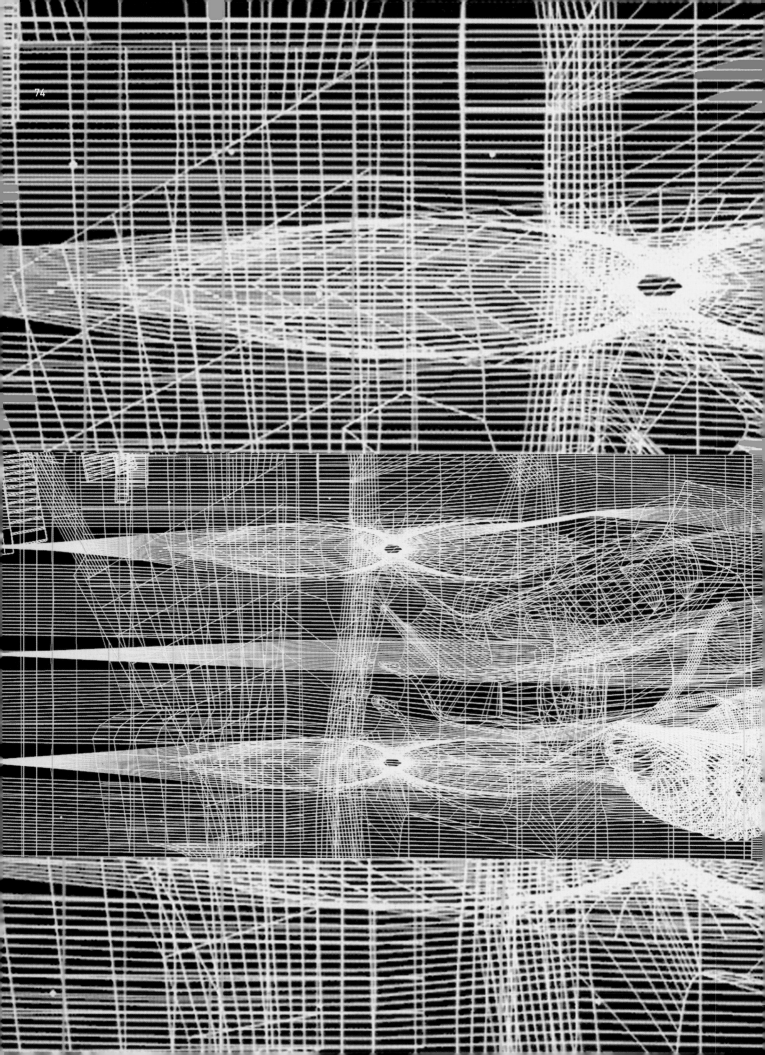

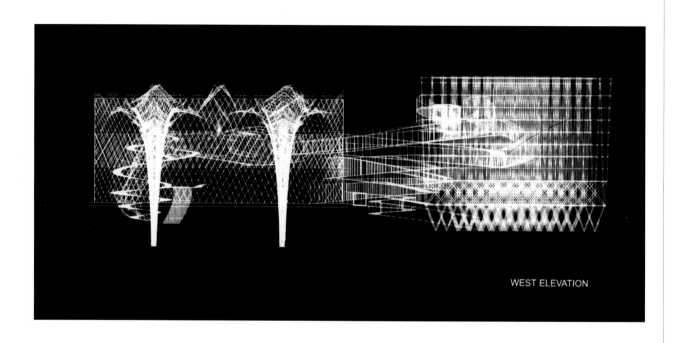

WEST ELEVATION

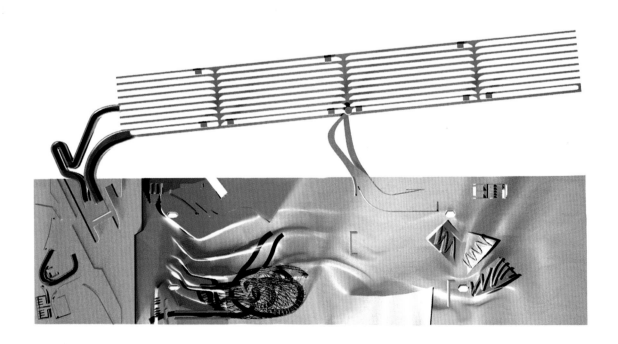

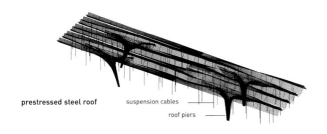

prestressed steel roof   suspension cables

roof piers

geodetic spiral ————————

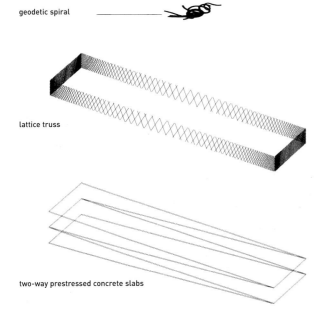

lattice truss

two-way prestressed concrete slabs

KANSAI LIBRARY:
elevation (opposite, top)
first floor plane (opposite, bottom)

exploded structural diagram (top)
second floor plane (bottom)

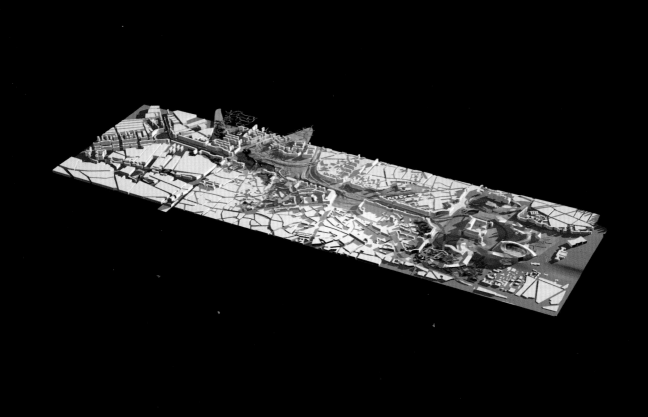

BUCHAREST 2000, ROMANIA

Urban Planning Competition, 1996

'What is torn – torn must remain', Wittgenstein.[1]

Despite the passing of Romania's totalitarian regime, scars – manifestly visible and invisible – deface the centre of her capital city. The singular and violent nature of this transition, along with the built legacy of the Ceausescu regime – an inflated monumental urbanism – enables the persistence of structures of meaning that in the context of the post-industrial West belong to an almost forgotten time. The eagerly awaited reflowering of the material and cultural life of Bucharest is inevitably attended by monuments to recent tyranny.

Proposals, therefore, that would attempt either to restore the pre-1980s fabric, or conversely, those which propose a radical elimination of the 1980-89 Ceausescu projects would, in their respective ways, engage in utopian models that are wholly inadequate to the situation at hand; the former, by indulging in a nostalgia for a lost city – a city which in any case is so rent by the 1980-89 intervention that no amount of local restoration would repair the wound nor take into account the unprecedented planning demands presented by future socio-economic realities. The latter, while obviously unrealistic in terms of economics (it is unlikely that the city would be inclined to demolish the 1980-89 projects), is unfounded in perhaps more profound ways. Elimination of the monuments left by the recent history amounts to a totalitarian gesture in itself (whatever the style of its replacement), for it suppresses a history that is still very much alive and for that reason still very much a threat. Rather than attempt to replicate an erased fabric, the proposal seeks to invigorate central Bucharest through a series of infrastructural grafts, that while responsive to the existing context – none of the buildings of the 1980s intervention will be touched – inherently produce their own patterns of growth.

THE HIGHWAY – AN ACCESS THAT IS NOT AN AXIS

The plan endorses the production of new urban morphologies that would locate themselves at the zones of systematic conflict between a proposed high-speed vehicular loop and the contexts it crosses. The loop traverses the length of the palace axis – effectively linking areas laid waste by the 1980s interventions. More importantly, it will serve to revalue the totalitarian effects of the axis through a two-fold process: firstly, by destituting its symbolic trajectory with the 'lateralising' capacities of the highway (along with large systems derived programmes, such as shopping malls); and secondly, by tempering the brutality of the highway by burying it under a mounded park that will run the entire length of the axis. Thus the axial mounded park will counter the totalising condition of the axis in two ways: by the landform continuously deflecting paths and views away from the axis; and by creating an intimate landscape that would promote strolling and small group interaction over forced parades. The success of the proposal depends upon the capacity of these morphologies to actively mediate between global systems of transport and exchange and specific sites in the city. The morphologies must therefore, of necessity, derive from and be affiliated with the global highway system, yet be responsive to the context. In this sense, they are globally driven rather that contextually driven.

The revitalisation of Bucharest depends upon the powerful forces of cultural and economic transformation engendered by a cosmopolitanising infrastructure rather than by a provincial contextualism.

1   Quotation from Ray Monk, *Ludwig Wittgenstein: The Duty of Genius*, Penguin Books (London), 1991, p87.

aerial view (opposite)
People's Palace (top)
nightview of palace and
convention centre (middle)
proposed infrastructure:
coarse and fine systems (bottom)

annotated site plan (overleaf)
aerial view (pp82-83)

SEGMENT A
HOUSE OF PARLIAMENT

1 Museum/theatre complex
2 Commercial street/parking complex
3 Mixed use commercial and residential
5 Auditoriums
6 Library layer
7 International conference centre
8 Stadium
9 Stadium facilities building
10 Parking structure
11 Convention centre, exhibition halls
12 'Cholla forum' museum & theatre
13 Hotel complex
14 Commercial /residential fabric
15 Switchback building - commercial use
16 Shopping mall
17 Heliport
18 Underground parking

SEGMENT B
LIBRATII BOULEVARD - PIATA UNIRII

19 Medium-rise hotel and restaurant/entertainment
20 Parkspace

SEGMENT C
PIATA UNIRII

21 Patriarchy Hill Park
22 Historic preservation zone

aerial view

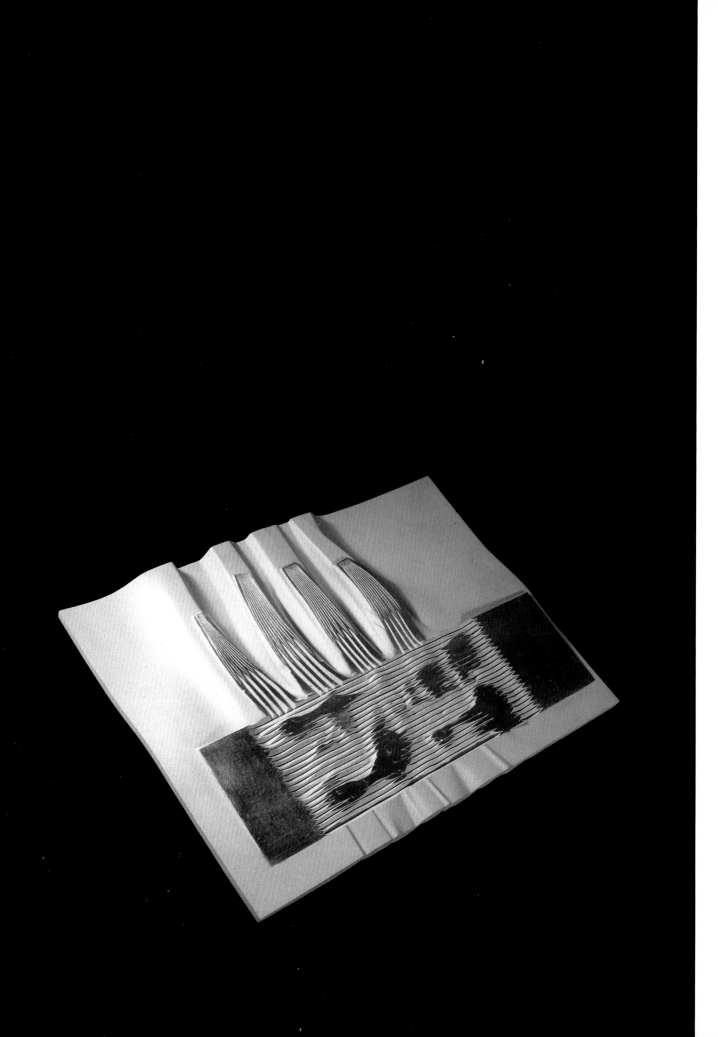

WATER GARDEN

Project, 1997

The architecture of the garden, more than that of mere buildings, has historically encompassed the full range and implications of man's engagement with the material environment. A more or less permanent feature of Western architecture, from classicism to the various modernisms, has been the almost ineradicable idea that there exists a permanent and unchanging essence behind the world of appearances; that such essences universalise themselves in fixed, simple geometries and timeless typologies. Time thus makes itself evident within two distinct yet related schemata: first, architecture as a stable and unchanging framework within which, and against which, the temporal unfolds; and second, how the mutable nature of character can be made to approach or deviate from a certain ideal. In eighteenth-century French topiary gardens, for example, where the relative crudity or refinement of simple geometrical forms in plant materials serve to establish the norms and limits for their speculation and enjoyment, these schemata are locked in a perpetual circularity with permanence set against change, and vice versa. If, however, we shift our focus from such static models of nature and architecture to the materially based paradigms of dynamical systems then far more possibilities are opened up. Time is no longer understood to be prior to, above, or separate from the material world but is engendered by, and finds its particular incarnations in it.

Nature, then, is less a 'creation' to be speculated on than an inventive and modifiable matrix of material becomings. While it might be argued that abandoning the two schemata outlined earlier leads to forms of naturalism, where nature in some sense is allowed to take its own course (with the assumption that natural development without human intervention will display its own creativity and inherent virtues). It will be shown, however, that there exists a fourth possibility that, contrary to a passive naturalism, requires intensive artifice towards the production of natural effects. Nature, it will be argued, will of its own inertia tend towards developments of increasing stability and banality. A salient and intensive architecture thus requires the deliberate production of instability in order to produce novelty. Here, it will be necessary to set aside the nature/culture dialectics and focus instead on those processes that establish transverse developments across these regimes. The French philosopher Gilles Deleuze coined the concept of the 'machinic phylum' to refer to the overall set of self-organising processes in the universe.[1] These include all processes in which a group of previously disconnected elements (organic and nonorganic) suddenly reach a critical point at which they begin to 'cooperate' to form a higher level entity. Recent advances in experimental mathematics have shown that the onset of these processes may be described by the same mathematical model. It is as if the principles that guide the self-assembly of these 'machines', for example, chemical clocks, multicellular organisms or nest-building insect colonies, are at some deep level essentially similar. The notion of a 'machinic phylum' thus blurs the distinction between organic and nonorganic life.

THE GARDEN: FIXED POTENTIALS/FLOWING MEDIA

A literal testbed for these conceptions was suggested by Jeffrey Kipnis who, in the project's formative stages, collaborated with us on a design for a water garden at his residence in suburban Columbus, Ohio. The project was then developed in two directions – Kipnis pursued the development of the garden in the earth/substrate as a series of linked pools; our proposal moved towards the development of a garden as a grooved laminar system in a concrete slab. In outline the garden consists of a furrowed-concrete slab measuring 7.3 x 21.9 metres

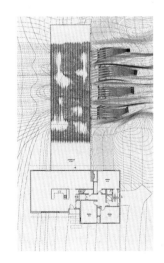

computer-generated laminated object model (LOM) finished with aluminium-zinc alloy spray (opposite)
site plan (top)

(24 x 72 feet), containing a laminar system of twenty-four parallel grooves, each with a variable ogive cross section measuring an average of 45.7 cm (18 inches) from point to base. This material geometry constitutes the 'primitive' through which a hierarchical series of global and local transformations – warps, dimples and folds – are expressed. Extreme and unstable configurations in the topology are essentially built into the concrete substrate in order to express them in the vital media (water, soil, plant materials, and chemical salts) of the 'flow space' above.

The topology of the substrate induces transformational events that introduce real discontinuities in the evolution of the media flowing on it. In such topological manifolds the characteristics of the mapped media are not determined by the quantitative substrate space below it but rather by the specific singularities of the 'flow space' of which it itself is part.[2] This means that the 'dead' yet intensive geometry of the grooves excites material and/or biological novelty in the media. In literal and instrumental fashion, multiform gradients in the geometry 'diagram' and trigger the gradients of growth inherent in natural systems and yield a prodigious, if only partially manageable, field of blooms.

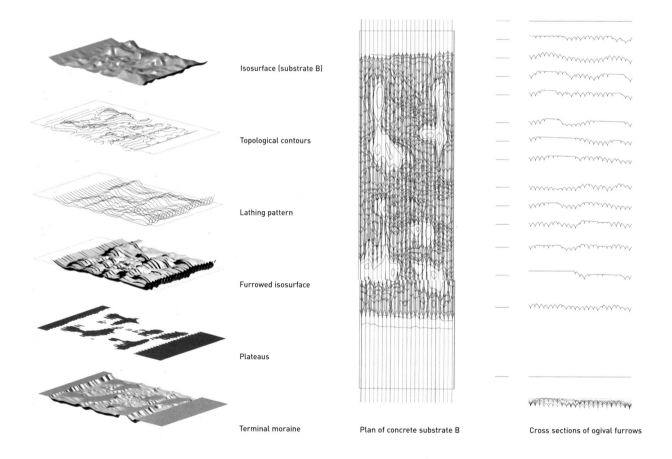

Isosurface (substrate B)

Topological contours

Lathing pattern

Furrowed isosurface

Plateaus

Terminal moraine

Plan of concrete substrate B

Cross sections of ogival furrows

1   Manuel de Landa, *War in the Age of Intelligent Machines*, Zone Books, MIT Press (Cambridge, Mass), 1994, pp6–7.

2   Sanford Kwinter, 'Landscapes of Change: Boccioni's Stati D'Animo as a General Theory of Models', in *Assemblage* 19, MIT Press (Cambridge, Mass), 1992, p58.

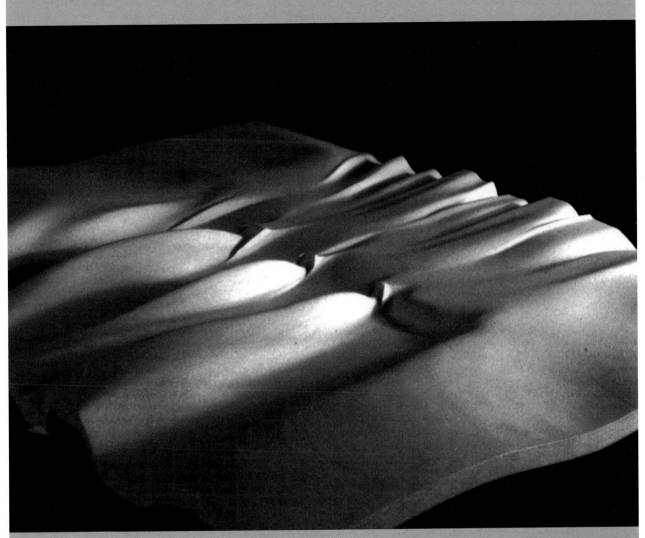

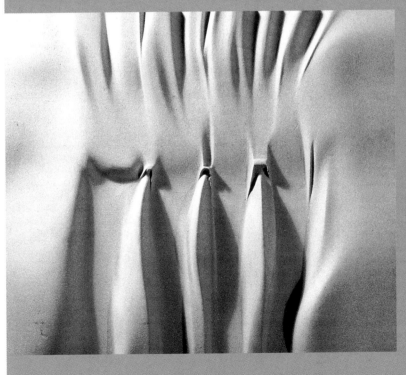

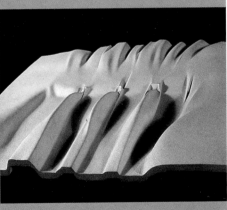

WATER GARDEN:
studies of interlacing earth bermes

water level study (overleaf)

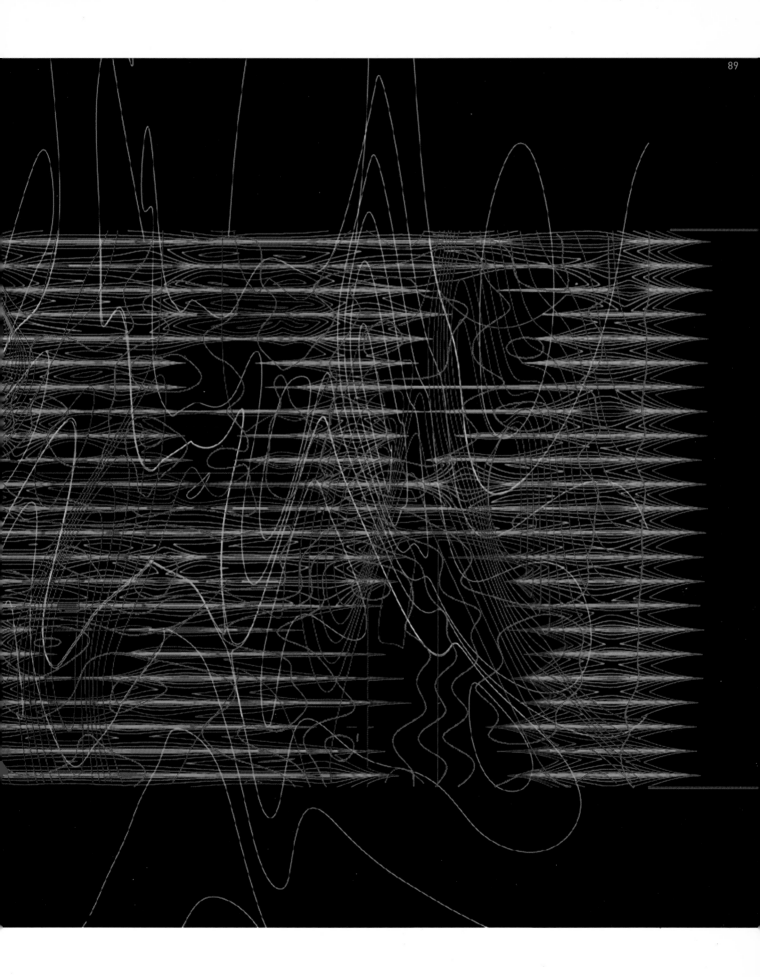

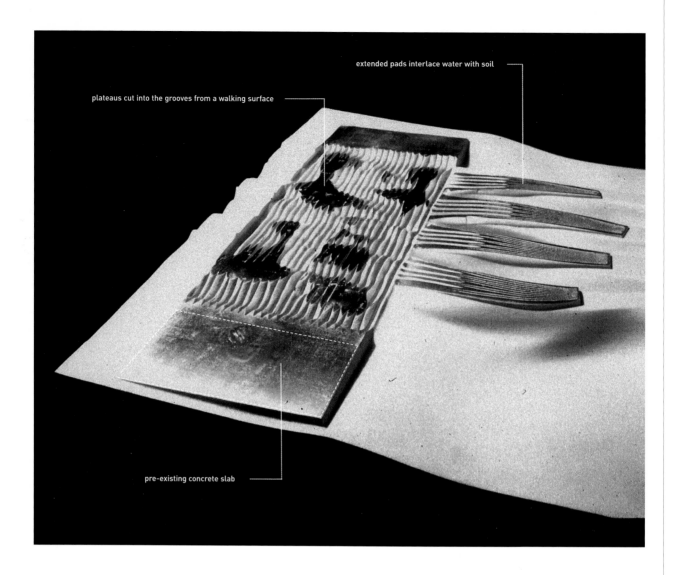

extended pads interlace water with soil

plateaus cut into the grooves from a walking surface

pre-existing concrete slab

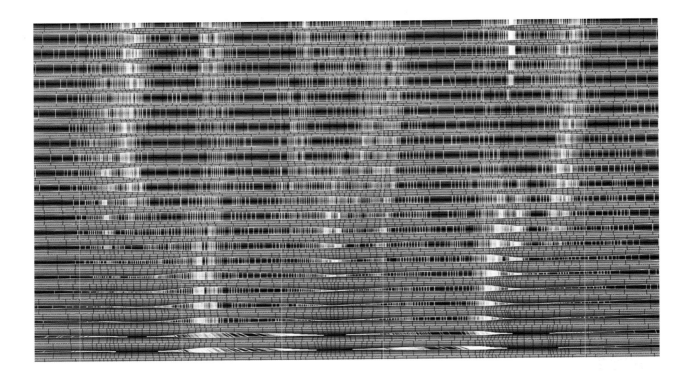

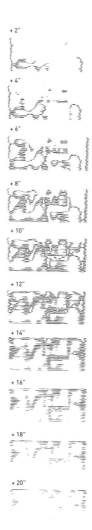

+ 2"

+ 4"

+ 6"

+ 8"

+ 10"

+ 12"

+ 14"

+ 16"

+ 18"

+ 20"

WATER GARDEN:
laminated object model (opposite top)
computer-milled formwork and
concrete tile (opposite bottom)

density map of flow space (top)
water level studies (left)

WORKS

1984   Rear Garden, Brechner Residence, Sands Point, New York

1985   Independent Commision for Wooden Tower, Yeshiva University Museum, New York City

       'Garden of the Heterocite', Villa Farsetti, Project for Venice Biennale

1986   Gardens and Terrace, Mirvis Residence, Riverdale, New York

1986-87   Bronze element from Mnemonic Theatre for the Garden of Mr and Mrs Milton Brechner, Sands Point, New York

1987   Métier à Aubes (*chaise-longue* and reading machine), Sands Point, New York

       Parking Lot and Ventilators, Courtyard, Dan Brechner Co, Floral Park, New York

       Garden and Courtyard, Wolf Residence, Sands Point, New York

       Garden and Courtyard, Starr Residence, Old Westbury, New York

1986-88   Globe Theatre Project, Bankside, London

1988   Proposal for Marna Anderson Folk Art Gallery, New York City

       Design of Study, Shiller Residence, Briarcliff, New York

       Shadow Theatre, Globe Theatre Project, New York

1989   Drummers Collective, Space and Video Offices, New York City

       Schwartz Residence and Studio, Taos, New Mexico

       'The Icarus Project', Marul Co Ltd, Kyoto, Japan

       Japan Tex Exhibition Space, Marul Co Ltd, Tokyo

1990   Venice Gateway, Competition Entry, Venice Biennale

       Aktion Poliphile, Entry for House Competition, Wiesbaden, Germany

       Croton Aqueduct Study, with Stan Allen (First Phase), New York State Council on the Arts and

       The Architectural League of New York

1991   J Jadow Residence (Landscape Design, Pool, Pergola, Swing Structure), Millriver, Massachusetts

       Cohen Residence (Landscape Pool), Tennafly, New Jersey

       Brechner Residence (Landscape, Garden, Drive), Sands Point, New York

1992   Croton Aqueduct Study, with Stan Allen (Second Stage Completed), Graham Foundation, Chicago, Illinois

       Boros Residence (Equipment Enclosure, Pergola, Fences), Sands Point, New York

       H Jadow Residence (Pavilion, Bridge, Pool, Pergola), Millriver, Massachusetts

       Levinson Residence (Garden), White Plains, New York

1993   Apartment and Furniture for Mr Leonard Brechner, New York City

       'Camera Lucida', Installation for Apartment Window of Dr and Mrs Zimmerman, New York City

1994   Cardiff Bay Opera House, Competition Entry, Wales

       'Head Start', Competition Entry, East Windsor, New Jersey

1995   Geodetic Bridge, Cohen Residence, Tennafly, New Jersey

       Yokohama Port Terminal, Competition Entry, Yokohama, Japan

1996   Kansai Library, Competition Entry, Kansai Science City, Japan

       Spence Center for Women's Health, with Debora K Reiser, Wellesley, Massachusetts

       Bucharest 2000, Urban Planning Competition, Romania

       D Sklar Residential Loft, New York City

1997   Water Garden (Project), in collaboration with Jeffrey Kipnis, Kipnis Residence, Columbus, Ohio

Water Garden, topographical detail

1997   Spence Center for Women's Health, with Debora K Reiser, Bethesda, MA

1997   Spence Center for Women's Health, with Debora K Reiser, Wellesley, Mass

1997   Proposal, The Brasserie Restaurant, Seagram Building, New York City

1997   Proposal, Student Center, Illinois Institute of Technology, Chicago, Ill

EXHIBITIONS

1982   One Man Show of Drawings (Jesse Reiser), The Cooper Union School of Architecture, New York City

1985   Invitation Entry for Villa Farsetti, Venice Biennale

       'The Art of Celebration', Yeshiva University Museum, New York City

1987   Group Show, John Nichols Gallery, New York City

1988   'Table to Tablescape', Formica Corp, Chicago

       London Project, Globe Theatre Project, Artist Space, New York City

1989   'Form; Being; Absence', Griffin McGear Gallery, New York City

1990   'Aktion Poliphile', Royal Institute of British Architects, London, and Gallery ZB, Frankfurt

1991   Yale University Faculty Exhibition, Princeton University and Miami of Ohio University

       'Ero/Machia/Hynia House', National Institute for Architectural Education, New York City

       'Architects and Artifacts', The Society of Arts in Crafts, Pittsburgh

1992   'Machines d'Architecture', Cartier Foundation, Paris

1993   Yale University Faculty Exhibition

1994   'Cardiff Bay Opera House', Architectural Association, London

       'Kyoto Future Space', Kyoto Art Museum, Kyoto, Japan

1995   'Eidetic Images', Architectural Association, London

       World Architecture Triennale, Nara, Japan (MAT)

       'Reiser+Umemoto', Miniseries, Columbia University

1996   'Reiser+Umemoto', The Cooper Union School of Architecture, New York City

       'City Speculations', The Queens Museum, Queens, New York City

AWARDS

1975   Thesis Award, School of Urban Planning and Landscape Architecture,

            Osaka University of Art, Osaka, Japan (Nanako Umemoto)

1976   Gold Medal for Painting, New York State Awards (Jesse Reiser)

       Gold Medal for Silversmithing, National Scholastic Art Awards (Jesse Reiser)

1981   Second Prize, IAUS Columbus Circle Competition (Reiser + Umemoto)

1984   Prix de Rome in Architecture (Jesse Reiser)

1988   Gregory Millard Fellowship in Architecture, New York Foundation for the Arts (Reiser + Umemoto)

1990   Design Arts Grant in Architecture, National Endowment for the Arts (Reiser + Umemoto)

1992   Project Grant, New York State Council on the Arts and The Architectural League of

            New York (in collaboration with Stan Allen) (Reiser + Umemoto)

1993   Graham Foundation Grant, Croton Aqueduct Study (in collaboration with Stan Allen) (Reiser + Umemoto)

PUBLICATIONS

1983   Jesse Reiser, projects in 'Work of the Cranbook Architecture Studio', *Parametro* (Bologna), August, pp16-18

1985   Jesse Reiser in Daniel Libeskind, 'The Maledicted Style' in 'Beyond Style', *Precis*, no 5, Columbia University

            Graduate School of Architecture (New York), pp28, 30

       Catalogue of the Venice Biennale, Electa Publications (Milan), p134

       Catalogue of the Annual Exhibition, American Academy in Rome, p24

1987   'The London Project', *Blueprint* (London), February, p38

       Young Architects Issue, *Progressive Architecture* (Cleveland, Ohio), June, p94

'Last X-ray Picture of Architecture', *New Observations* (New York), July, p19

Victoria Geibel, 'Harbingers of Change', *Metropolis* (New York), November, p53

1988   Globe Theatre Drawings, *Assemblage*, no 5, (Cambridge), Spring, cover and inside cover

'Métier à Aubes', *House & Garden*, August, p25

Victoria Geibel, 'Reiser+Umemoto: Reflections in Steel', *Metropolis* (New York), April, p30

1989   Kikan Toshi, 'Globe Theatre Project', *Urbanism Quarterly* (Tokyo), July, pp10-14

'Shadow Theatre', *Sculpture Magazine* (Philadelphia), August, p32

Gavin Hogben, 'Reiser+Umemoto' in 'American Authenticity', *Architectural Review* (London), February, pp59-61.

'The Globe Theatre', *The Pratt Journal of Architecture*, vol 2, Rizzoli (New York), pp50-54.

'Globe Theatre', *The London Project*, Princeton Architectural Press (New York), Chapter 2, pp1-13

Jesse Reiser, 'Thesis Project' in *Education of an Architect*, The Cooper Union School of Architecture,
        Rizzoli (New York), p280

1990   'Reiser & Umemoto', introduction by Daniel Libeskind, *A+U* (Tokyo), November, pp38-61

Aaron Betsky, 'Globe Theatre Project' in *Violated Perfection*, Rizzoli (New York), pp159-60

Aktion Poliphile (exhibition catalogue), Forum fur Architektur und Design (Frankfurt), 98-101

1991   Paul Rosenblatt, *Architects and Artifacts* (exhibition catalogue), Society of Arts in Crafts (Pittsburgh, Penn), pp37-38

Patricia Philips, 'Reiser & Umemoto' (exhibition review), *Art Forum*, September, pp136-37

Reiser+Umemoto, 'Hynerotomachia Ero/Machia/Hynia, House', *Assemblage*, no 13 (Cambridge), Winter, pp88-105

Robert Somol, 'Domesticating Assemblages, *Assemblage*, no 13 (Cambridge), Winter, pp60-71

Alain Pélissier, 'Machines D'Architecture', *Techniques et Architecture* (Paris), December, p78

1992   Reiser+Umemoto, *Machines D'Architecture* (exhibition catalogue) Fondation Cartier (Paris), pp38-41

Chantal Beret, Exhibition Review of Machines D'Architecture, *Art Press* (Paris), April, p23

Paola Antonelli, Exhibition Review of Machines D'Architecture, *Abitare* (Milan), May, p111

M Iwashita, 'Young Architects in New York', *Space Design* (Tokyo), September, p72-77

1993   Croton Aqueduct, Greg Lynn (guest editor) in 'Folding Architecture', *Architectural Design* (London), February, pp86-89

Jesse Reiser, 'Semiotexte Architecture – Facade Writing', *Semiotext(e)* (Los Angeles), Fall, p28-30

David Evans, 'A Plurality of Words', *AA Files* (London), no 24, pp89-90

1994   Tsuyoshi Matsuhata Raaum, in 'The New East Coast Movement', *Space Design* (Tokyo), August, pp40-43

Tsutomu Niijima, *Terminal Architecture Syndrome*, Parco Press (Tokyo), pp43-44

1995   Reiser + Umemoto, 'Computer Animisms: Reiser+Umemoto Cardiff Bay Opera House',
        Assemblage, no 26 (Cambridge), pp26-37

Jesse Reiser, 'Some Notes on Geodetics', *Architecture +* (Berlin), October, pp55–57

Elizabeth Suerbeyeff Byron, 'Architects on the Verge: Reiser+Umemoto', *Elle Decor* (New York), pp254-55

Jesse Reiser, 'Post-Contradictory Practice' and Reiser+Umemoto collected projects, *World Architecture Triennale*
        (catalogue), Nara, Japan, pp152-65

Jesse Reiser, 'Post-Contradictory Practices and Reiser+Umemoto', *Space* (Seoul), pp118-25

1996   Stan Allen, 'Sites and Stations', *Provisional Utopias*, Lusitania, (New York), pp205-7

Georgi Stanishev, 'Take Four: Alternative Designs for the Cardiff Opera House', *World Architecture*
        (London), January, pp106-7

Andrew Benjamin, Reiser+Umemoto Exhibition Review, *Columbia Newsline* (Columbia), February, p8

Greg Lynn, 'Blob Tectonics', *Any Magazine* (New York), May, pp15-16

Anthony Freund, Design Pool Project, *Town and Country* (New York) June, p50

Nopadol Limwatanakul, 'Reiser+Umemoto: Cardiff Opera House', *Architectural Profile* (Thailand), July, pp78-85

Reiser+Umemoto 'Some Notes on Geodetics' and 'Cardiff Opera House'; and Andrew Benjamin, 'Not to Shed
        Complexity', *Fisuras* (Madrid), pp26-37, 46-59

1997   Reiser+Umemoto projects in 'Architecture After Geometry', *Architectural Design* (London), May/June, pp92-95

Reiser+Umemoto recent work, *Space Design* (Korea), forthcoming

Reiser+Umemoto Exhibition, *Columbia Documents*, no 6 (New York), forthcoming

Yokohama Port Terminal, *Journal of the University of Lisbon* (School of Architecture, Portugal), p8

Patricia Philips, 'The Water Project' in *City Speculations*, Princeton Architectural Press (New York), 1997, pp72-77

Jesse Reiser, 'Latent Tectonics in the Work of Tony Cragg' in 'Sculpture, Art and Design', *Art and Design*
        Profile no 55, Academy (London), pp76-83

1998   Manuscript and collected projects compiled in preparation for a book with Sanford Kwinter

CREDITS

MÉTIER À AUBES, 1987
Principals
Reiser + Umemoto
Metalwork
Jan Larson

VENICE GATEWAY, 1990
Principals
Jesse Reiser, Stan Allen,
Nanako Umemoto (RA Aum)
Assistants
Michael Silver, Maki Uchiyama

HEADSTART PRE-SCHOOL, 1994
Principals
Reiser + Umemoto
Assistant
Hideki Tamura
Computer Work
Sean Daly
Software
SoftImage

CARDIFF BAY OPERA HOUSE, 1994
Principals
Reiser + Umemoto
Assistants
John Kelleher, Jun Takahashi,
Taiji Miyasaka, Don Keppler,
Terry Surjan, Hideki Tamura,
Rhett Russo, Jason Payne,
Yama Karim

YOKOHAMA PORT TERMINAL, 1995
Principals
Reiser + Umemoto
Assistants
Yama Karim, Don Keppler,
Jason Payne, Rhett Russo,
Fadi Hakim, Lawrence Blau,
Khalid Abdulkarim
Computer Work
Sean Daly
Laser Cutting
Rawbeam
Software
Form Z

BUCHAREST 2000, 1996
Principals
Reiser + Umemoto
Assistants
Tod Rouhe, Rhett Russo,
Ali Rahim, Steve Chen,
Jose Sanchez, David Ruy,
Greg Merriweather

Thanks to Gateway Lab,
Columbia University

KANSAI LIBRARY, 1996
Principals
Reiser + Umemoto
Assistants
Yama Karim, Marco Studen,
Jose Sanchez, Robert Ayona,
Shigeru Kuwahara
Computer Work
David Ruy
Software
Alias Wavefront
Consulting Engineer
Ysreal Seinuk

BRASSERIE RESTAURANT, 1997
Principals
Reiser + Umemoto
Assistants
David Ruy, Jason Payne,
Jose Sanchez
Software
Alias Wavefront

WATER GARDEN, 1997
Principals
Reiser + Umemoto
in collaboration
with Jeff Kipnis
and David Ruy
Computer Work
David Ruy
Software
Alias Wavefront
Laminated Object Model
Era Industries